France ~ the quiet way

On the River Doubs, part of the Canal du Rhône au Rhin near Besançon

France ~ the quiet way

John Liley

Stanford Maritime
London

Stanford Maritime Limited
Member Company of the George Philip Group
12 Long Acre   London WC2E 9LP
Editor Phoebe Mason

First published in Great Britain in 1975
Reprinted 1977
Revised and reprinted 1980, 1983
Copyright © 1975, 1980, 1983 John N Liley

Set in 10/11pt Plantin by St Paul's Press Ltd, Malta
Printed in Great Britain by BAS Printers Ltd
Over Wallop, Stockbridge, Hampshire

British Library Cataloguing in Publication Data
Liley, John
   France, the quiet way.
   1. France – Description and travel – 1975-
   2. Boats and boating – France
   3. Inland navigation – France
   I. Title
   914.4'04'83   DC29.3

ISBN 0-540-07402-0

Acknowledgement

Portions of this book have earlier appeared in *Motor Boat and Yachting* and are included here by kind permission of the Editor. I would also like to thank several friends for their help in compilation, most notably Michael Streat, Michael Peyton, Robert Shopland, Nicholas Hopkinson, and the staff of *Practical Boat Owner*, while Albert Barber, who contributed many photographs, also kindly drew the maps. Unless otherwise credited the pictures used are my own.

I dedicate this book to the many friends and helpers who made the exploratory voyages in *Arthur* so enjoyable; and to the lock-keepers, canal officers and boat people of France.

J N L

Also by John Liley :

Journeys of the *Swan* (George Allen & Unwin)

Inland Cruising Companion (Stanford Maritime)

Barge Country – an Exploration of the Netherlands Waterways (Stanford Maritime)

Contents

Appendix

Index

Maps, Marks
and Signals

A Boat for France

'Mr C S Forester is making what is perhaps a unique trip in an outboard motor boat throughout France, living aboard the whole time with his wife.'

Thus began an article in the magazine *The Motor Boat* of May 1928, with a brief introduction by the editor; and a couple of sentences later Mr Forester himself set out. His craft was the tiny *Annie Marble*, fifteen feet long and five in width. She had cost him £20, her fittings a further £15, and he shipped her out to Rouen through Messrs Carter Paterson.

Issue by issue his reports came in, sometimes with tiny photographs showing a lock on the Canal d'Orleans ('the sleepiest, shallowest, least-used canal in France') or the press of barges on the Seine. Later the accounts were published as books: *The Voyage of the Annie Marble* and then *Annie Marble in Germany*, before Forester moved on to Hornblower and the deeper waters in which he swam.

It is still possible to emulate Mr Forester, to float peacefully through the rivers and canals of central France. There are many different ways, although people today are often encouraged to travel too speedily, or in craft that are totally unsuitable. Having been the editor of a boating magazine myself, I have had the good fortune of first seeing the Continental waterways at other people's expense, before hunting down the right sort of boat for myself, giving up my job and then venturing abroad again for two seasons more extended than conventional holidays can allow.

In theory any vessel is suitable for the French canals, provided that she falls within certain generous clearances. In practice many pleasure craft are tediously awkward to handle, and seagoing boats in particular often fare badly inland, being too vulnerable during their encounters with standing masonry to bring any great job to their owners.

A steel barge on the other hand requires no fenders, other than a judicious tyre at a mooring to prevent any noises from awakening the slumbering crew. Such a vessel can endure the tow through a Continental tunnel, which is usually compulsory, with little more than a hollow bonging sound as she noses into a cupboard-shaped recess in the wall. She may be happily leaned upon by her 350-ton French counterpart, the standard *péniche*; she can be tethered against the sloping stone quaysides that are a French speciality, or may float against a lock wall on the River Yonne, also sloping, without mishap. The single screw is well protected from any boulders on the bottom, while the draft of such a vessel, when empty, is shallow enough to permit an approach to the bank.

It may be some comfort to learn that small and light boats are often the next best bet, being at least adaptable, and comparatively cheap. No boat is really cheap to run, of course, being much more complicated than at first appears – far more complex than a car for instance, and more directly comparable to the running of a house. Once this is understood the matter can be put in perspective and a barge, being durable and capable of withstanding rougher treatment, becomes more of a proposition.

My own craft *Arthur* is such a barge, built at Northwich in Cheshire in 1932, and for many years a regular on the Leeds & Liverpool Canal. Nowadays the Leeds & Liverpool is a leisure canal only, like so many on the English system, but in its working years it was a very tough waterway indeed, where the tradition, such as it was, veered more towards cloth caps and string around the knees than to the directly maritime.

Arthur is of a type known as a Leeds & Liverpool 'short boat', measuring 60ft overall and 14ft in beam. In keeping with the anti-romantic stance of their helmsmen, the short boats had names like *Edgar*, *Joe* and *Alf*; and *Arthur*, which when launched had first of all been given the name of *Mersey*, was in 1949 rechristened *Arthur of Skipton* by a carrier who named the boat after his son. Two later owners tried to rectify these North Country aberrations by calling the boat *Bertha*, but I never really liked it. A name is very important to a boat; as a lady friend once said, pointing to the dented bows and the iron stem, offset like a boxer's broken nose, 'he looks like an Arthur somehow'. And to me he does. I have never happily called *Arthur* a 'she' ever since.

It is possible today to buy a boat in a showroom, and if this is centrally heated and there are bright and jolly posters around the walls, the salesman's job is very much easier. The buyer, on the other hand, should imagine what things will be like when moored against a gasworks and in the pouring rain. Even more to the point, he must picture his family and his friends sitting down below in such conditions, for almost all boats stay moored for longer than they are under way, and it can rain even in the South of France.

It is often useful to see a boat under disadvantageous conditions, and so it was with *Arthur*. Our first meeting was at the Public Wharf in Leicester, an unsavoury patch beside the Grand Union Canal, which like so much waterside property at that time had decayed into a medieval squalor. There were pig-bins and mud, broken bricks, and in a tumbledown shed a rotting pile of leather scraps. It seemed possible to catch the plague.

An unflattering situation is helpful when buying a boat: *Arthur* in the rain at Leicester.

It was winter, and the time of the International Boat Show, an indoor jamboree staged with much glossiness and swagger back in London's Earls Court. It was difficult to imagine a more pointed contrast, for here was a boat made of iron, and very old iron at that. On closer inspection the material proved to be steel, but a steel unlike that used in boatbuilding today, tougher and less likely to rust away. A timber superstructure had been added above the hold and covered in roofing felt, a much underrated substance in the boating world, but scarcely a material to conjure with aesthetically. There is something about a boat with a past, all the same, quite apart from the fact that a new barge of this type would cost ten times as much to build. Those subtly buckled deck plates, reminiscent of a generation of clogged feet; those bows, a memorial to a thousand collisions with locks and bridges, were all in a sense a consolation.

When I explored the boatman's cabin in the bow, the atmosphere was irresistible, and the very stuff of what the boat salesman should be offering. For here was a cast iron coal stove, still in working order, with an ornamental pattern upon its face. There were iron pans and implements, including a toasting fork, and among the lockers

The bow cabin stove

opposite an old pair of boatman's gaiters, gently fossiliz-ing in a drawer. On each side was a bunk, entered by climbing through a sort of picture frame. Within lay a private world, from which already I could imagine myself gazing out at the glowing embers of the fire.

The owner and hopeful vendor was a friend of mine, Mike Streat. It is not a good idea to do business with friends, but barges in England are in fairly short supply, and most of the other boats I had looked at were either rotten or rusted through. Visiting the purveyors of hulks is a sobering business. Almost inevitably the weather is miserable; there are Alsation dogs, and the owners tell pointless fibs. Corrosion and nailsickness vie for the des-truction of the hull and all therein, and there is little to promote confidence on the part of the buyer. I had found one other boat in decent condition at around £1000 minus engine, but her hold was cavernous and defied conversion save as a housing estate. Her owner had sworn on the telephone that she was ideally suited to the 14ft locks nearby, but fortunately I got there before him and measured the vessel's beam for myself: it was 15ft 8in.

The most obvious alternative is to buy overseas, but the project requires fair resolution and much ready cash. The advantage of having a boat near home is that she can be worked on in comparative leisure, and the prepara-tions spread over years if needs be; while at a distance it is a matter of conducting maintenance and repair by proxy. This usually involves a boatyard, and these can be very expensive. Holland is the traditional country for small barges, and by diligent enquiry it is possible to track one down; but in the short term the project costs much more money.

There is one particular snag about a British boat: if she is to go to France she must be capable of crossing the intervening sea. And here romance overcame good sense, for a canal barge is not at all suited to seagoing in any weather, while predicting conditions can never be certain. It was difficult to believe that those battered bows would ever really point down the Grand Canal d'Alsace, or look the Eiffel Tower in the eye, but the concept was difficult to resist. Although I have had some seagoing experience, it is easy to overlook the might of the ocean when not actually fighting for survival upon it, and I resolved to run that particular gauntlet when I came to it.

If a boat is comfortable and agreeable to live in, there is much to commend it. In the hold of the *Arthur* there

The hold of a 'short boat' converts well into cabin accommodation. *Arthur*'s main saloon is roughly fourteen feet square and has four bunks in addition to a sink and cooking equipment. The superstructure is of timber covered in roofing felt and the windows are a standard type supplied for caravans.

group of friends, I stumbled about in a space reminiscent of the gunroom on a man-of-war. Stacked all around were the paraphenalia of canal travel: shafts, hammers, mysterious hooks, a bamboo pole with, for some forgotten reason, a pan tied to it, bundles of cord and cable, and furtively concealed behind a cupboard full of paint, a chemical toilet.

In the engineroom a mass of piping permitted a water ballast tank to be flooded, the bilges to be pumped, and the engine cooled. Blunt instruments hanging from a rack testified to the stiffness of the taps. The engine itself was a modern marine diesel, quieter and less bulky than the exotic single cylinder unit it had recently replaced. A canal boat needs very little power; in fact the traditional single horse was often quite adequate. *Arthur*'s engine is a 45 horsepower BMC diesel, consuming one-half or perhaps three-quarters of a gallon in an hour.

We went for a trial run. Watched by the two elderly ladies who constituted the permanent garrison against marauders, we cast our ropes from the foul quayside and edged the fifty yards towards the lock. For the next hour or so we were stuck there, with a sunken oil drum wedged beneath one of the gates. There is little help to be had in such incidents, for lock-keepers are a race long since departed from most of Britain's canals, and one does things oneself, winding open the sluices, or 'paddles' as they are known in England, with an iron key or 'windlass' and leaning on the balance beams to open the gates. Whenever these processes are impossible, it is quicker for the willing crew to resolve the matter for themselves, usually with a long boathook or shaft.

The English canals are in a far worse condition than their Continental counterparts, so that they require a lot of raking and prodding. In France, as I already knew, the lock chambers are much bigger, and there are keepers to look after them properly. Our struggles provided some incentive to get across the English Channel and try them.

The general handling of a boat is an important factor in its success. Quite contrary to popular belief, a big heavy boat is often easier to manage than a light one, being less susceptible to wind and the effects of going astern, which

are four additional berths and a long galley, all combined within the large main cabin. In the interests of economy the after portion is covered over at a lower level. Mike had alluded to this in letters –, 'Why not a 'tween-decks party for tall men broken on the wheel of toil?' Gravely, with a

A trial run. Buyer and vendor pole off a shoal.

as little as possible, and as a result empty craft of many kinds tend to bowl down the water like pie dishes. The solution is to provide ballast, as much of it as possible, and many of today's small boats could so benefit.

It is for this reason that *Arthur* has a ballast tank in the stern. Mike had also added twelve tons of industrial blue bricks under the floorboards in the hold, so that the broadsiding tendency was much more under control and only showed itself if we went into a corner too fast. Once you got the hang of it handling was quite easy; I decided that I liked the boat very much.

An evening around the stove clinched the deal. As the coals glowed and our kneecaps gently charred, I knew that here was a boat with not only the practicality required, but the romance as well. I made Mike an offer, and he accepted.

When you buy a boat you are supposed to do so 'subject to survey'. By this you agree to buy on the understanding that the vessel is in the condition represented. You then bring in a surveyor, who looks at the boat rather as a doctor examines a footballer up for transfer. The system has its pros and cons. Most boating magazines get tearful phone calls from people who have bought unwisely. I once had one from a man who had spent £11,000 on what proved to be low quality firewood; and there was no redress. Certainly with a wooden boat a survey is well worth having. Here the surveyor is in his element. He pokes the stem with a needle; he drops a keelbolt (quite often involving the digging of a hole in the boatyard floor) and he taps the hull judiciously with a hammer. But the advent of fibreglass has made these processes awkward, while to survey steel the customary method is to drill the hull full of holes in order to verify that the plates are thick enough for such apertures not to appear naturally. Afterwards the holes are sealed up again by welding, taking care not to miss any out.

Some people claim it possible to measure the thickness of a barge hull by whacking it with a hammer and judging the ring of the steel, but in my own experience the interior frames affect the resonance. Squatting beneath a whale-

can make single screw boats spin around like tops. The River Soar, which lay not far downstream, provided a deeper and hence more convenient area in which to assess *Arthur*'s own characteristics.

Arthur's tendency is to broadside on a bend. Many commercial craft do this, the traditional narrow boats of the Midland canals being almost the only exception. Quite understandably, barges have been designed to trim best when carrying loads, it being the humblest prayer of their proprietors that they should work in an empty condition like hull in drydock, the idea of going over it all, inch by inch as is generally suggested, becomes totally awe-inspiring. In *Arthur*'s case it is akin to inspecting the ceilings of six large bedrooms, and at one tap every second it would take thirty-six hours to go over it in this fashion.

It had been the thought of doing all this, of necessity in a dock that was not available at that time, that had deterred me from buying *Arthur* 'subject to survey'. Not long afterwards, in the course of another abrasive voyage through Leicester, a hole had appeared in the bottom. It was only a small hole, about the size of one old penny, but it was a hole nonetheless. It took several seconds to admit it, before stopping the bubbling water with a wad of cloth. We had been forcing through ice at the time, and were additionally encumbered by the miscellany of baby carriage components, old TVs and gents' tailoring that lies on the canal bottom under the Leicestershire bridges.

Whether the hole was caused by ice thrown up by the propeller or the wreckage of an old parapet upon which *Arthur* had stranded it was difficult to say. Sooner or later the damage would have to be repaired, and, as is often the way, the only dock big enough was several miles distant. It was twenty-five miles away, just inside the old Erewash Canal at Long Eaton off the River Trent.

In the meantime the hole could be plugged with a piece of plywood wedged down with sawn-off blocks and finally sealed with clay from the lockside. It is the common experience of boat hire companies that a holidaymaker's first instinct is to hastily abandon ship at such moments, leaving the boat and all posessions to slowly sink. But this need not be so. I have seen a 1300-ton Rhine barge with a gash in the bow temporarily plugged with plywood, and there have been boats going around the English waterways for years with leaks plugged up with wedges, with the ends of broomhandles, and with string; but there are not many owners who actually prefer to run that sort of a ship.

The journey back to the dock demonstrated one or two other truths. There was a sudden thaw, and much rain. With the first spots of each downpour, the crew would thunder forward to leave the helmsman in lonely isolation at the stern. Cheery faces grinned back from the hatchway yards ahead, beaming over mugs of cocoa, while smoke billowed from the stove beyond. The bridges of the Grand Union are not high enough to permit a wheelhouse, but those on the Continent are, and some sort of steerer protection was going to have a high priority. On boats up to *Arthur*'s size a tiller provides a much more exact means of steering, and also allows the sudden corrections in course that may be necessary as a vessel sheers through mud. The disadvantage of a tiller is that the steerer cannot so easily sit down, nor is he in the comfort of a cabin.

With the thaw came floods, which lowered the bridge clearances even further. Thus the stove chimney altered shape a little, and a friend of mine, Albert Barber, who had been recklessly piling on wood, emerged as a changed and gibbering man, half-smoked and convinced he had been struck by lightning.

The dock at Long Eaton witnessed many spectacles. I now had to pay for other people's time. If his overheads were taken into account, a skilled workman cost upwards of £2 an hour (he costs even more now). When you have followed a welder around all morning while he weighs up the job, remembers distant tools and decides that he will need a lad along to help him, it is not very long before a little taxi-meter starts whirling in your brain. Mercifully, Ray the welder could work very quickly once the work had begun, but it became apparent at a very early stage that the more amateur preparation that could be done in advance each day the greater would be the saving.

As soon as *Arthur* had been pulled into the dock, and the water drained off, I had looked at the hole itself. Obviously the steel in that area was thin, and there was a clear-cut reason. The rule of the road on canals is to keep to the right. Canal people never say 'port' or 'starboard', and rarely 'bow' and 'stern'. And so, whether loaded or empty, it is a barge's back end that lies deeper in the water, and the right-hand side of it that rubs most on the shelving canal bottom. I now know that this is the place to look at most closely in any old working boat. At the time it was

In dock for repairs and improvement. Welding the bottom
of a barge involves quite a crawl.

important to discover how widespread the damage was
while still safely in the dock, and so I rained a hail of blows
upon the plate in question, fully expecting it to crumble
before my eyes. But it did not yield an inch, and after
several minutes of hammering I gave it up.

There is one device by which a steel hull may be
inspected without boring it full of holes. This is the ultrasonic tester, which has been developed for oil pipelines,
warships' hulls and other apparatus which does not take
kindly to being drilled. It is used rather like a doctor's
stethoscope, by placing a little sensor on the spot selected,
and then reading off the thickness on a dial. These devices
are expensive, even to hire, but I managed to borrow one

through a friend. The results were gratifying. Forty
years of wear and tear had affected the hull remarkably
little. It is a fact that old steel is a good deal more durable
than recent steel, the methods of production having
changed. I marked out the one area for replating and
arranged for one or two doubtful welds to be renewed.

At weekends, with many an injury, we stacked and re-
stacked the ballast in the wake of the electronic tester.
There were floorboards everywhere, bricks in all directions. Helpers wobbled like gnomes in the decked-in hold,
or teetered on chairs in the disarranged main cabin. In
Ray's track voluntary labour applied black goo to the
exterior. Occasionally, when the river rose, it would come
back up the drains and into the dock itself, to float away
tins or rust forgotten tools

A retired boatman called by, to insist that this wasn't
Arthur we were working on at all, but an old boat called
the *Aire*. I stared once again at the files I had inherited,
at the reams of correspondence from the Registrar of
Ships, a gentleman who needs to be precisely satisfied
regarding every change in ownership before bestowing
the debatable benefits of British registration. There was
a picture in an old British Waterways magazine dated
1950, showing *Arthur of Skipton* proceeding loaded, and a
friendly letter from James Glover, coal merchants of
Bingley, concluding '. . . I send my Best Wishes to you, and
to the success of boat *Arthur*. She was always a good boat.'

It seemed that we had been treated to a typical red
herring of the canals, where every ex-boatman likes to
tell you that your boat once was his. It was important to
get the name painted on once again, not upon the hull, as
tradition demanded, for here it becomes rubbed and be-
slimed upon lock gates. Instead it seemed preferable to
have a cutwater, a raised plate that could deflect spray
and sport the name in the manner of the French barges.
Such a modification, if properly arranged, can also provide a sighting point for the steerer, a mark by which he
can judge when the bow is at the far end of a lock.

Ray welded it up; then Albert, who includes a typo-
graphical training among various accomplishments,
pointed out that the name deserved careful consideration,

Using an ultrasonic tester to check plate thickness in the hold.

and perhaps tapering letters. It was to take many months before an acceptable typeface could be evolved on the office enlarger. In the meantime the boat travelled anonymously, save when we experimented with chalk.

It was now late spring. From purchase to renewal, which had also included an engine overhaul, *Arthur* had occupied four very intensive months. The welding over, the hull a gleaming black, we let the water back into the dock. *Arthur* lifted from the blocks, ready to be floated out.

Any programme such as our own involves putting to sea, sooner or later. In *Arthur*'s case this meant a preliminary voyage down the East Coast and into the Thames Estuary. There was much work still to complete, and with a boat this is always most effectively done near home. It seemed logical to take *Arthur* down to London where I lived and which is, roughly speaking, on a line between Long Eaton and France anyway.

There are in fact canals between Long Eaton and London, but a barge by loose definition is 14ft wide or more, whereas the canals of the English Midlands were built for 'narrow boats' which only measure 7ft. It is

one of the commandments of the English waterways that a narrow boat should never be referred to as a barge, and it is symbolic of the daftness of the English canal system in general that a narrow boat cannot go on the Leeds & Liverpool Canal because it is too long, while a barge from that canal is too wide to come south.

There is a maddening stretch not far south of Leicester, which is a 'narrow canal' for a mere twenty-one miles; nor is it narrow for all that distance, for the bridges and tunnels along its length are of barge width. Only in the locks at either end, ten at Foxton, and seven at Watford Gap, just by the M1 motorway, is this really a narrow canal. If as an alternative the voyager can make it into the Nene, by way of a short jump across the Wash, there stands a further barrier at the upstream end, a single flight of locks at Northampton, all 7-footers.

Like others in this predicament, I have toyed with mustering my friends, anaethetizing them with drink, and persuading them to haul the boat up the towpath on rollers. Other schemes sprang to mind. Someone suggested a helicopter, but upon reflection thought it would have to be a big one, as *Arthur* weighed over thirty tons.

We mused on road haulage, but Mike had mused on that before me. He had been quoted £800. On each of many hypnotic journeys up the motorway for working weekends, I had visualized *Arthur* straddling two lanes, with a motorcycle escort front and back and about sixty-eight wheels beneath. It seemed a bankrupting prospect.

The only thing left was the sea. Mike had enquired about a tow. Having been quoted £900 plus, he had remarked on how nice it was that humour still remained in business correspondence and shelved the project. In my turn I rang and wrote to agents about shipping as deck cargo. I learned a lot about cranes and the lack of them, their expense if there were some, and that there was no longer any regular shipping service between the Humber and the Thames anyway. So that was that: we would have to do it ourselves.

The most southerly jumping-off point from the wide canal and river system of the North is at Boston in Lincolnshire. It is 180 nautical miles from London, with

The motor short boat *Our Girls* at Burnley in July 1927.
Loaded capacity would be 50 or 55 tons of coal.

the engine and other equipment to show themselves, while at the same time providing a glimpse of *Arthur*'s homeland, the Leeds & Liverpool Canal.

The Northern waterways are monumental, and some even have the merit of being deep. Within a fortnight *Arthur* had braved the lower Trent, with its disconcerting tidal wave, the 'aegre', which slops along the lower reaches through Gainsborough. Although not dangerous, the aegre, which looks like a small roller coming up a beach, gave us a turbulent few minutes off the village of West Stockwith. We had visited the Stainforth & Keadby Canal, which passes through the grassy outback near Goole, and also the Aire & Calder, one of the few British waterways with modern equipment. The Leeds & Liverpool itself alternated between stygian industrial gloom and glorious reaches across the Pennines, with the canal winding tightly among the moorland pastures before dropping down again to the mill towns of Lancashire.

We had picked a big wooden sherry barrel from the water during the ascent, and now sported this as a cult object on deck, as it proved too big to stow below. From the very moment of its installation, ostensibly for drinking water, it had proved itself a passport to good-natured conversation, for even a bystander who does not know a short boat when he sees one can think of something to say about a barrel. Even when empty it seemed worth its place on board as a generator of bonhomie, and an alleviator of tension among anglers.

From the occasional maintenance man and bystander on the towpath we learned more of the Leeds & Liverpool ethos, of the days when one man worked a short boat alone, leaping off at the lockside and operating the long gear lever by twitching a length of string. We sailed across the mighty embankment at Burnley and lurched through the shoals of Blackburn. At length *Arthur* reached the top of the twenty-one locks at Wigan, notoriously the hardest in the country.

And here we stopped, for after raking out countless gates, after the extraction of numberless tyres and polythene sacks from the propeller blades, there seemed little point in continuing through yet another industrial area

few ports of refuge on the way. We would be skirting the coastline, which is the course often, and quite erroneously, believed to be the safest. In practice hugging the coast, as it is usually termed, is akin to staying close to the ground in an aeroplane. It is the ground, generally speaking, that you are not too anxious to hit.

Since sea areas Humber and Thames are no great respecters of the Leeds & Liverpool tradition, any boat coming down the North Sea – or for that matter any sea – must be prepared most thoroughly. I was also loathe to leave the waters of the North without having looked at them, so I planned a short canal trip first, lasting about a fortnight. This would enable any basic shortcomings of

Working a lock. After closing all gates the water level is adjusted by winding open sluices or 'paddles'. This particular lock is on the Erewash Canal near Long Eaton and the paddles are in the gates. The boat is of the narrow beam type common to the Midlands canals and necessary for passing from North to South.

when at the end of it all we would be obliged to turn around and retrace our steps. For the error that I constantly make on the canals is going too far in the time available, and when this happens I do not see very much. It is easy to become a Rommel of the waterways, lured ever forward by maps. It is a temptation one sometimes manages to fight.

The journey back put us under further scrutiny. Northern voices carry, and as it is one of the delusions of those upon bridges that anyone below is bereft of hear-

ing, one learns an awful lot about oneself, some of it most original.

The marked feature of these commentaries is the lack of knowledge displayed of how a canal lock works. While many people nowadays can change a car wheel, or identify a Ferrari Dingbat at fifty paces, comparatively few realize that lock gates can only be opened if the water levels on each side are exactly equal, or that it is the paddles which let water into or out of the lock chamber, either through culverts or through gaps in the gates themselves. All locks work on basically the same system: the boat is enclosed within the chamber by gates ahead and behind; water is then let in or out to float it to a new level. In detail, however, the process can be confusing. Gates and mechanisms both vary, and in practice their only point in common is that they are universally stiff.

Perhaps the best known of all the Leeds & Liverpool locks are the five at Bingley, which incorporate a principle which is also to be found from time to time on the Continent. In practice there are eight locks at Bingley, but it is the five-lock staircase, the Five-rise, that is deployed so enthusiastically on country calendars and the covers of ladies' journals. In a staircase the top gate of one chamber also serves as the bottom of the next, so that no stretches of water intervene, and the view from the top is precipitate. The main shortcomings of staircases are that they waste water and that craft cannot pass each other within them. If one boat has just descended, another must let down several lockfuls in order to climb. Sometimes intermediate reservoirs are provided, filling and draining deviously through further paddles and as a result the pitfalls are legion, so that even in England a canal official tends to hover in the background to sort out the more spectacular floodings.

The Aire & Calder Canal Navigation which links Leeds with the Humber is more on the Continental pattern. Here the locks are remotely controlled, with hydraulic pipes and gantries and a variety of other devices tacked onto the stonework of an earlier era. The keepers sit loftily in little signal boxes, and although amiable and inclined to shout cheery witticisms, they take no part than to arrest it. The 'brakes' of a boat are provided by engaging reverse gear, and stopping can take some time. With single engined craft there is also a complicated phenomenon known as the 'paddle-wheel effect' which causes the boat to sheer in one direction whenever the engine goes hard astern. Sometimes it can be a help, as when gliding in at an angle towards a lock wall (the paddlewheeling propeller will then both stop the boat and pull it straight), but every helmsman or woman, however experienced, can get things wrong occasionally; provided both boat and surrounding property are strong enough, this does not matter too much.

At the big locks of the Aire & Calder we would try to ease off very early, putting the engine out of gear and gliding to a halt well upstream, since each of these locks, when filling, has a considerable 'draw', when water flows down through the paddles.

Once in the lock, someone would get off with a bight of rope and drop the end over a convenient bollard. And there *Arthur* would hang, perhaps with the engine pushing gently forward again to keep the rope tight and to hold the boat in against the wall. In the tight fitting locks of

The 'staircase' flight at Bingley. Here the five lock chambers directly connect through gates and there are no intervening stretches or 'pounds' in which boats might pass. Staircases are also more wasteful of water, but when built were sometimes the only easy means of overcoming sharp changes in level.

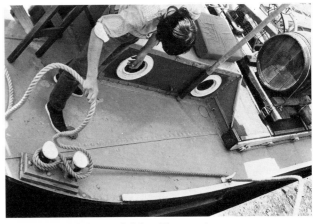

Making fast with figure-of-eights. Three turns of the rope generally suffice, and if no final tuck, hitch or knot is made the line may be released when in tension.

in the brandishing of ropes and the general manoeuvring of craft: that is the boatman's responsibility.

The secret in most boat handling, so easy to preach about if less easy to practise, is to take all complicated manoeuvres slowly. It is far easier to resume progress

Leicester or the Leeds & Liverpool no ropes are necessary at all, but without them here it was possible to be swilled around. When descending in a small lock, the main concern is that the stern should not catch on the sill, an Eiger-like ledge beneath the gates. In the bigger lock chambers ropes must be watched and if necessary adjusted, lest the boat should once again be left suspended as the water level drops. A most useful talent is that of flicking ropes off the bollards before departure. Many boatowners prefer to double ropes around a bollard and back on board instead but I am not particularly keen on this myself, as there is more adjustment involved and the lines can become entangled.

We diverted into the Yorkshire Ouse, another tidal river which whirls along muddily towards the Humber and with great gusto on the ebb. The trick is to descend at this time, taking care not to become stranded as the river becomes shallower. If the calculations have been accurate it is possible to arrive at the mouth in time to catch the next flood tide up the Trent. Some way back up the Trent lies Torksey, the junction with the Fossdyke Canal. By means of the Fossdyke, which is said to have been cut by the Romans, it is possible to reach Lincoln, and beyond that, by means of the River Witham, Boston and the open sea.

At Torksey I took stock. There had been several mechanical incidents on the way. A vital nut had released itself on our first day out in Nottingham and the propeller, instead of acting in reverse, had merely twiddled itself part way out of the boat. We had hit some bottom gates a portentous wallop, filling the sink with toothbrushes and decimating the crockery. With John Sheldon, a narrow boat owner of long standing and a man well versed in marine idiosyncracy, I had reassembled the reduction gearbox. On the Leeds & Liverpool itself I had steered too near the bank while exchanging gesticulations with a trainload of football enthusiasts, and ominous knockings had been heard from the engineroom as a result. Part of the clutch pressure plate had broken away through the shock of the propeller hitting a large stone. A man from the makers had come 150 miles the next day, and

In some of the shallower English canals a boat drawing three feet can rub on the bottom for mile after mile, and the propeller is particularly vulnerable to rubbish. On this occasion it had picked up steel binding tape from a packing case.

after seven hours' heavy labour had replaced the broken part.

Gearbox dismantling is the sort of task that is all too glibly described in the instruction book. In practice it involves standing on your head in the hottest and spikiest part of the vessel. Bolts sheer; you cut yourself; oil seals defy extraction. The gearbox itself proves to weigh several hundred pounds and must have been assembled by Strang the Terrible in a rage. Out of every pore it oozes oil.

The engaging thing about professional mechanics is that they can perform in a trice and without damage a job that takes me all day. That the replacement of this one component took a professional an entire afternoon indicates the intricate nature of the job. We had helped as much as possible by carrying things, had undone several nuts in advance in order to speed the process and had made a gasket from an old Admiralty chart. When it was all over and everyone could stand up again, I developed a fresh mania about gearboxes and their sensitivity, and as a precaution against heavy hands we shortened the operating lever with a hacksaw.

Having braved the humps and bumps of the Leeds & Liverpool and the currents of the Trent and Ouse there were no other reasonable tests to inflict. The next chapter in the saga would involve putting out to sea.

Waterways of England, and *Arthur*'s route around the coast.
Thin lines indicate 'narrow' canals.

A Coastal Passage

The essence of any sea trip is preparation. If something cannot be done before you set off, it is extremely unlikely to be settled *en route*. Anyone who does not prepare soon discovers this, for just as the crew are feeling sick and the wind ascends like a funicular through the Beaufort Scale, the boat will spring a leak, the lockers will burst open and shower the captain with processed peas, and the engine will decide that it prefers diesel oil to suspended rusty sludge. Everthing must be lashed down beforehand. Shelves must be cleared, drawers wedged or taken out; anything that could conceivably move, including ballast, water tanks, stove and gas bottles, should be lashed as if to withstand a giant's hand. Above all the engine must be in running trim.

It was for these reasons that so much had been done beforehand. One job among many had been scrubbing a forty-year accumulation of rust from the fuel tanks (making a hole in the process, one of several extremely depressing moments). Something like eighty per cent of engine breakdowns among small craft are caused by dirty fuel, so a number one priority is a sound set of filters and several spares. Having looked at the engine manual, a volume made even more paradoxical by an even layer of grease, I bought other bits and pieces: a thermostat, spare injectors, pipes, gaskets, wire, sealing fluids, bolts, nuts, and the tools with which to fit them.

As a sea boat a sound metal barge like *Arthur* has no problems in respect of stability, being beamy enough, and also strong enough, to withstand any amount of racking and pitching. A more important consideration is whether anyone might stay aboard in the process, for the steering position is almost indecently exposed, and the deck, even if sealed over, is generally low enough for foaming wavetops to sweep across with suitably reckless abandon. I sorted out plans for a rudimentary cockpit, and earmarked ropes for lifelines.

In the meantime it is always a good idea to get as near as possible to the sea itself, so that when the prayed-for patch of settled weather arrives time is not being wasted at the locks or waiting on the whims of swing bridges. And so one weekend we moved the boat to Bardney in Lincolnshire, subsequently to become a haven for pop festivals, since it was miles from anywhere, albeit within striking distance of Boston. Both the Fossdyke and Witham cut across the beetfields in a series of straight-line jags. The route from Torksey is not the world's most inspired, but since the land is flat it was possible to swing the compass on the way, taking bearings of Lincoln Cathedral.

The compass had needed a lot of thought, since there was enough iron around the boat to distract it from its main duty of pointing north. The best plan seemed to be to set it as high as possible above the deck, and so I chose a hand-bearing compass, which you look into the side of rather than onto from above, and I stuck it up at eye level, mounted on a wooden post. Compass 'swinging' merely means aiming the boat in a number of known directions and comparing the compass readings with the true ones. I took the true readings from the Ordnance Survey map, using a plastic protractor, and by the time we had crossed the unexpected lake at Lincoln and squeezed under the fourteenth century housing beyond, the compass was more or less weighed off. Fortunately all OS maps are inscribed with the magnetic variation for the area, the difference in angle between the 'true' north, the North Pole, and the magnetic north, which is what compasses point at and which I find it convenient to think of as a large lump of iron ore somewhere at the top of Canada.

I labelled the resulting table in several different ways in order to prevent myself from subtracting compass error when I should be adding it. The next task was to lash together a rudimentary cockpit out of old planks as gesture of protection towards the helmsman.

Obviously I hoped never to encounter an angry sea, but the ocean rarely does what you want of it, nor will it stop misbehaving when required. When all else fails there is one final resort: a boat is as good as her ground tackle, and so I had purchased a huge ex-Admiralty anchor. With it came thirty fathoms of chain and a hundred feet of nylon rope, all of which might prevent contact with the coast *Arthur* would be hugging, should we be caught in an onshore wind. In a similarly pessimistic vein it was necessary to check over flares, lifejackets, lifebelts and extinguishers, plus the pump and buckets. I also hired a liferaft.

Having perused the charts so many times that the navigator's eyes have worn grooves in the paper, and having contemplated tide tables with an equal obsessiveness, all that remains on a voyage is to depart. Back in London I had become a transistor addict. The shipping forecasts are broadcast four times a day, though not necessarily at the most convenient times of day, since they get wedged between such all-essential programmes as the Early Show and Sports Report. In order to figure out what was going on it is necessary to listen to all the forecasts, possibly for weeks. Each must be instantly recorded on paper, for it is a feature of these sessions that the strength and direction of any wind is forgotten within moments. If written down, however, the details of one transmission can be kept for comparison with reports given at the end of the next, and so changes in the weather pattern may be confirmed.

Arthur's crew on this occasion was made up by myself and two stoical friends from the world of publishing, Colin and Keiren, both of whom were inexplicably keen to come along. We put ourselves into a state of instant readiness, or so we thought, but the right forecast, when it came along, nonetheless caught me on the hop.

It was now the middle of September, statistically a good month for calms, but too near to winter for us to turn down any good opportunities. Alas, on my last visit to Bardney I had done what the careful captain should never do. I had disabled the boat by sawing through the fuel line, in anticipation of buying an extra filter. And so, when the radio signalled us to be away, we were stuck, for no-one stocked the necessary pipe unions, least of all the London depot of the filter makers. Standard fuel fittings may in fact be purchased from the suppliers of Calor gas, who use the same kind of thread, but it was several months before I discovered this, and in the meantime I was lucky to run down the right bits at a garage accustomed to servicing heavy lorries. Thus somewhat late we hammered down the Witham to Boston, still mechanicking and lashing down every bit of gear in sight.

The problem with Boston is that the lock there is ridiculously short for what the British conceive as big boats. It may then be used only twice on every tide, when the levels become equal and when for a brief moment craft can float straight through. Waiting for this kind of thing adds yet another straw to the burdens of premature old age. I lay on my bunk in the evening twilight listening to an insistent trickle through the gates and trying to ignore the glare from the street lamps on the bridge. Keiren said it was like waiting for one of those cisterns that never quite fill.

Such is the atmosphere before a voyage. A lifetime passed and then, quite suddenly it seemed, we were out of the lock and racing down on the ebb through a narrow

The Boston Grand Sluice separates the tidal and non-tidal portions of the River Witham. Its intricate arrangement of gates permits only craft of 59ft and under to pass through in the normal way. Larger vessels must wait until the salt water outside makes a level with the river.

the main channel in order to clear the mouth of the Wash before the tides turned against us. Local seamen have a knack of endowing their primary hazards with awe-inducing names. A lightship with the cheering title of Roaring Middle marked the end of the passage between the mudbanks that were now becoming visible as the tide dropped further and further. Ahead lay Sunk Sand, Gore Middle and The Woolpack, all cheery shoals on which to founder.

I am not a good skipper; I show my apprehensions too clearly, which a good captain should never do. When we picked up a piece of wood in the propeller my feet must have left the deck as I jumped at the noise. One advantage of a high-mounted propeller, however, is that you can sometimes reach it with your bare hands. In a reflex action I stopped the engine, hopped over onto the rudder, and reaching down to my armpit in the sea, extracted not only the timber but a raggedy length of rope from around the boss. Luckily it was calm enough to do this, for the alternative of disconnecting the shaft within the boat and trying to wind off the rope from there is a fraught and time-consuming business, probably involving anchoring in the bargain in order to avoid going aground.

There usually comes a time when you are glad to have tied everything down. Dawn found *Arthur* wallowing; we had missed the tide and were stuck just clear of the Wash, slogging across a shallow patch known as the Burnham Flats and with a lolloping chop to stop us. *Arthur* rolled in his own froth, making about two knots forward.

The forecast was for light winds, blowing from the north, and the last report on the radio had put things at around Force three, although we seemed to be running into a little bit more. I switched on the radio. 'Humber, Thames', it said cheerily, 'winds northwesterly, Force six to seven, locally eight. And that was the origin of my part in a campaign to get the forecasts broadcast at times nearer to their issue by the Meteorological Office. On an inhospitable shore we were faced with a wind in the Last Trump category.

My memories of other Force eights, 'yachtsmen's gales'

gut between the houses. Just ahead lay blackness, and the sea.

Any estuary can be eerie. The Wash, with its bleak and lonesome saltings, its absence of visible comforts, is just such a region. Keiren, Colin and I, enshrouded in oilskins, lifejackets and safety harness, talking little and smiling not at all, could have been moon men, cautiously stepping onto a hostile planet.

It was nearly midnight. *Arthur* pushed forward at about five knots, still riding on the ebb and aiming to reach

At sea in total calm. The compass is mounted at eye level
in order to be as clear as possible of magnetic interference
from the steel hull and deck.

Out on deck again, I found the sea distinctly rougher.
Water was surging from under the cover of the ballast
tank and I kicked myself for not foreseeing that this
could happen. Of all times, this was one when we needed
the propeller more or less under the surface. The pump
could just keep pace with the rate at which the water
rushed out, and I reflected upon the irony of having to
pump water into a boat at sea.

It flitted briefly across my mind that I ought to have
been taking pictures of this epic, recording for ever
the sight of Keiren and Colin wrestling with the tiller and
braced against the tilting sea. A journalist often allows
disaster to take place while he goes on photographing it,
but this I have always found difficult to do. I once missed
a dramatic shot of a man who had leapt from a sinking
boat because I was one of several people who were clinging
to his wrists at the time. Likewise it now seemed a derelic-
tion to forget even for a few moments that I was navigating, and to devote myself to photography instead.

We had made the Bridgirdle buoy, five miles to the
northwest of the entrance, its name confirmed in heavy
lettering as it rolled in the waves. With the tide now helping once again, *Arthur* altered course and made inshore.
Reckoning our own speed through the water at about
five knots under increased power and with the wind
astern, and adding a further component from the invaluable tidal atlas, it was possible to lay a rudimentary
course for the Wells outer marker, shown on the chart as
a black buoy.

Reaching this was simple enough, but it was easy to
miss the next one, a much smaller mark the size of a
turnip, almost lost between the wave tops. The fixed
beacons stood like pylons among the breakers, plainly
nowhere near the channel, and the water around the
nearest was chopped and confused in a way that showed
hardly any depth at all. It was now shortly after high
water; the ebb was beginning, the incoming seas starting
to break. Hitting the throttle to its peak, we surfed in. If
there had not been sufficient depth we could have floated
the boat on adrenalin.

Suddenly *Arthur* was in calm water between two pro-

and otherwise, are of large lumps of water heaving into
view with an extreme vigour, and no barge would have
liked them. Keiren at the helm reacted with a single word.
I remember concentrating as never before on charts and
tide tables, and realizing that, thanks to our delay, we were
off the small port of Wells, the only haven of any consequence for a very long way. It was exactly the right
time, and the only time, for entry. All that remained
was to locate the place and get in, but that could be tricky.

The chart showed a big expanse of sand, with a note
about small black buoys and beacons. The *Cruising Association Handbook* had it in greater clarity, but unhappily
it had been written a decade before and sands, alas, change
more frequently.

tecting spits of land. We fumbled our way up the long creek that followed with only six inches or so beneath us, as we later discovered, for the inner markers were insignificant and I missed them completely in the euphoria of being in. Even as we anchored the wind creaked up another octave to blow the spray from off the wavelets. By now the bar was foaming.

Wells is an exhilarating little town. The line of buildings on the quayside put on a cheery front to offset our gloom at having fallen short of London. But I wondered all the same if *Arthur* was to stay there all winter, snapping at the mooring every time the tide came in. In demented dreams I visualized the iron plates dissolving through the continued immersions and dryings. Salt water is ferocious stuff, particularly when oxygenated, and I was already conscious of the rampant corrosion that is generated by such conditions. At low water we would march about on the rock-hard sand to stare at the propeller shaft bearing or tumble into water-filled craters among the saltings. While Keiren trailed across this primitive landscape in search of driftwood for the stove, Colin and I would take out the little plastic dinghy, purchased from Mike Streat as an afterthought and already invaluable as a ferry across to the quay where we did our shopping.

If Wells was awkward to get into, it looked almost impossible to leave. At low water a wiggly channel carved its way across the sands, the buoys marking only its general lie, and not the details. Coasters often came at high water to unload the fertilizer that blew like snow across the moorings, but how they made it across the bar remained a mystery. It just did not look deep enough. At low water I would walk out among the beach-ball carriers and families hunting for winkles, in order to sketch it all for future reference.

We kept on listening to the forecasts, writing down each one in order not to forget it. And it was with a now-or-never feeling that *Arthur* finally left, with the promise of light southwesterlies. With these I reckoned we would be in shelter as far as Great Yarmouth, and we would be picking up a further forecast on the way which could decide whether or not we should put in there. A gasket

had been made from roofing felt to stop the ballast tank from spilling; fresh food had been loaded; the waves had decreased to a popple.

This time the forecasts were correct. The English Channel sea areas were already calm and, as a generalization, whatever they are getting the southern North Sea areas get later on. And so it proved: Thames and Humber became calm too. We held a mile or two off the Doctor Doolittle shores of Norfolk, where pine trees and dusky beaches precede the high cliffs of Cromer. A local fishing boat, built like a walnut, came purring by with a row of jolly faces on board. The atmosphere was altogether more optimistic than in those tentative first hours out in the Wash. By the time we were off Great Yarmouth there was little doubt that we should go on, although the tide at that point was fierce enough to hold *Arthur* virtually stationary for a whole two hours. Once it had turned again, however, our progress was swift. A coaster of the Everard company rumbled by in the dusk as we altered course in the dog-leg between the shoals off Lowestoft. We lit the navigation lights again and worked out how the buoys and lightships would come up in the night.

A rudimentary system of three hour watches had been agreed upon, with the man at the tiller waking either of the other two if help were needed. Additionally I was to be woken myself if none of the various markers in our path showed up as predicted. Lest we should find ourselves at close quarters to any shipping I laid out a powerful lamp for shining at the bridge of any oncomer, and asked to be called for that contingency too. No self-respecting helmsman will run down a naked light, but there is some risk of not being seen at all, for lookout systems on merchant ships are sometimes slack. We carried among our flares several white ones, which do not signify distress, but which are valuable in warning off ships when all else fails. Officially they are disapproved of, but there comes a time when your own wellbeing must be put first.

It was difficult to conceive of disaster on such a sea. The water had become calmer even than the Trent or Soar, with the loom of each light visible for many miles. Southwold, Shipwash and the sombrely entitled Sunk

The sands of Wells. This small harbour may be entered in favourable conditions at or near high water.

'Winds light, variable' in the Thames
Estuary. It rarely comes as calm as this.

in a bellowed conversation, one that was closed for the
weekend. It was another sixteen miles to the other Grand
Union entrance at Brentford. There was just time to make
it, under Tower Bridge, past Lambeth, Westminster and
Putney and into cosy river territory again, with pubs and
double-decker buses as close as the ship we had passed
the night before.

Brentford approaches the Thames diffidently in a semi-
industrial jumble, but beyond the jousting sailing dinghies
and a small group of lighters stands the entrance to the
Main Line of the Grand Union Canal, by which Birmingham may be reached, and for those with boats that are
small enough, Foxton, the River Soar and the Trent. We
had reached fresh water again. It seemed a long time
since leaving Leicester.

Light Vessel all came and went, each exhibiting its own
distinctive group of flashes as on the chart. It became, if
anything, even calmer, so that the sea looked like glass, a
rare but much appreciated condition. By dawn *Arthur* was
plodding past the Barrow, one of many sands that radiate
from the mouth of the Thames, and upon which, in tougher
circumstances, many a good ship has foundered.

We had tied in very neatly with one of the strongest
flood tides of the year, one that was to take us all the way
from the Barrow up to Brentford, whooshing us through
London at an express speed within thirty-six hours of
leaving Wells. Coming down on the last of the ebb, an
array of coasters and sewage ships had passed, bound
respectively for Continental ports or the dumping grounds
in the estuary. We saw the armada of anglers off Southend,
then almost before we knew it *Arthur* was past Gravesend
and the wharves of Tilbury. A lighter had sunk and the
huge rolls of paper it had carried were drifting like depth
charges just beneath the surface. We missed one by inches,
then realized we were off the Regent's Dock, the theoretical entrance to the canals once again, but as I learned

The end of a sea trip. Saturday afternoon at
Putney.

The Final Preparations

Getting my own boat ready for France took over two years in all. In addition to the tasks already described there were some heavy sessions at a new mooring in Marylebone. Finding a safe place in which to leave a boat is not easy in an English city, and London's boating facilities, in particular, are a long-standing disgrace. Even the Thames tends to be separated from the general public by stone ramparts and floodwalls, and the great legacy of docks and quays is now being wasted in dreary developments that hardly stimulate life on the river at all. On the Regent's I had discovered a few select spots, sanctuaries in a world of Hogarthian squalor and neglect, and by pressing my case many months in advance I had been fortunate to gain a place at one of them. It lay just east of Little Venice in Paddington, a pool in the canal which in recent years had become an area of elegance and an estate agent's dream.

Arthur and I got to know the area quite well. The towpath, recently thrown open to visitors, attracted many enquirers. People would rap on the hull to verify the material, or press their faces against the windows. Mike had taught me a series of devastating responses to such curiosity, but I never had the nerve to use them and generally resorted to pulling the curtains instead. Water buses would surge past, parting the ropes of the unwary, including our own, while a firm of contractors demolished a remarkable row of cooling towers alongside by the simple expedient of attaching a bulldozer to the lower structure

and driving it away. A hail of planks descended upon various cabin cruisers alongside while a cloud of dry rot spores wafted slowly in the direction of Camden.

Down below a complete refurbishing of *Arthur*'s bow cabin demanded the descaling and painting of an acre of steel, and the tailoring of thirty-seven individual sheets of plywood in order to refurnish it. In removing the old lining Arch, one of many helpers, spectacularly revealed a forty year accumulation of rust beneath the deck, much of which fell on himself.

The log became peppered with the recorded aquisitions: turps, paint, lavatory fluid, fuel filters, gasket goo, tinsnips, more lavatory fluid, eyelets, a billion metres of rope and string. Visitors arriving on board were as likely to find themselves consigned to the hold with a scaling hammer as to be entertained to tea. On fine days the hull was anointed with sticky, insidious black varnish.

Occasionally we would venture out on more trips, past the Zoo with its terraces of antelopes and sad little owls, or battling into the threatened Paddington Basin which branched off from Little Venice, and in which every conceivable hindrance to navigation had been mustered.

In the summer that followed *Arthur* ventured up through the crowded Middle Thames to the magical reaches above Oxford. In a more experimental mood we tried the Grand Union Main Line, once a trunk artery, and although in theory a narrow canal for much of its course, one that was equipped with 14ft locks all the way up to Birmingham.

The Thames at Lechlade, Gloucestershire. This is the generally accepted upstream limit of navigation for all save light craft. Among the trees in the background is the entrance to the Thames & Severn Canal, now derelict, and the large round tower was once one of the lock-keepers' cottages.

Arthur stuck for six hours in a bridge not far short of Warwick, and a lot of other pleasure boat owners relieved their frustration at the delay by helping to chip away the towpath with heavy hammers. The struggle availed us of a few more miles before we were finally thwarted by a low bridge.

For the final working assaults I based *Arthur* out in a gravel pit near Rickmansworth. Many friends helped. The 45hp diesel which had stood up to so many abuses was overhauled yet again. We fitted a new exhaust assembly,

one of those outwardly simple tasks that takes four working days, once all the necessary pieces have been obtained. Holes were cut in $\frac{3}{4}$in plating, a new gas container was made, spares hunted down, and rubbish deposited on the Denham tip. With Bob Bennett, a cheery Bristolian, I littered the canalside with welding equipment and built a canopy framework to protect the steerer from the rain and, hopefully, the sun.

At 1970–72 prices it cost £1700 to run, equip and improve the boat in the two and a half years prior to departure for France. Of this, plate welding was the largest item at about £400, while the total sum also includes insurance costs at about £60 a year, and the various licences required for running on British waterways. Fuel is included also, but at that time was of little account, costing say £8–£10 for a fortnight's continuous use. Not included in these sums, however, is the cost of travelling to and from the boat on the many and various expeditions, and the price of food and drink when aboard.

The number of man-hours involved is beyond calculation. Suffice to say that there were a lot, some profitably spent, some less so. It took all day to replace a window broken by vandals in Paddington, because the type involved, a simple fitment intended for caravans, had changed in design since the first ones were installed. Among a vast general correspondence there was a Gilbertian exchange with the Thames Conservancy, who wanted £2 and 98 pence for replacing a chip of concrete removed when *Arthur* entered Pinkhill Lock. There was a more profitable one with the police regarding the dinghy, stolen near Rickmansworth and later found abandoned in the woods.

While such traumas were taking place I began organizing crews for the planned four month voyage in France. Unlike myself, most of my friends could only come for a week or a fortnight at a time, and a major operation developed in predicting where they might join. For many months beforehand I had been reading every book possible in order to find out which canals were the most attractive. Certain routes were out altogether, most notably the Rhône, which still ran too fast for *Arthur* to return again upstream, save by means of a highly expensive tow. I wanted, too, to end the year on the Canal du Nivernais, right in the heart of France, where I knew of a company which could look after the boat for me during the following winter.

Days were spent in drawing diagrammatic maps showing mileages and more to the point the number of locks, for there are many in France, spaced at roughly one every mile. From circulating among the multitude of fitters-out and lenders of encouragement it was possible to discover who wanted to come, and when. I tried to steer everyone into parties of no more than four or five and asked them to join on Saturdays. As a safety measure a fortnight was allowed for the trip to Calais, in view of the need to wait for settled weather.

Eventually a route was devised whereby, as each weekend arrived, the boat could be at the French equivalent of Banbury or Northampton, rather than the major canal intersections which, like those in England, are remote from other forms of transport. It might be added that although initially convenient, travelling out by car poses the most tiresome problems of retrieval which in my own experience cast a blight over an entire holiday, and it was for this reason that the schedule was primarily geared to the efficient French railway system.

Reckoning on 100-150 miles a week (a mistaken calculation, as it proved, for we should have aimed at very much less) it seemed possible to pick up people with a minimum of train changing, and yet to follow a course that took in some stimulating areas. A further consideration was the list of chômages, the stoppages for canal repair, which normally take place in mid-summer. They can last for as long as a month, and they need to be avoided. I had obtained a schedule of these from the French Tourist Office in London, and although some sensational emergency chômages would compel a few changes in plan, it was possible for those returning to distribute news of these disasters in time for outgoing crews to head elsewhere. Mike gallantly volunteered to operate the Arthur Information Centre with the idea of coordinating these endeavours, and I distributed a sheet bearing everyone's address and telephone number, plus an emergency contact in France.

I am often asked how long it takes to cross the Channel. In practice the actual journey between England and France was the least part of the matter. It is the preparation, and the voyage to the jumping-off point that takes the time. Arthur's passage from Brentford to Calais took three ebb tides, or two and a half days, if an overnight stop in Ramsgate is taken into account.

There were six aboard for this ultimate journey, which was once again preceded by much calculation and the recording of forecasts. There is a considerable difference between leaving from the Thames than from some coastal harbour, for only gradually does the vessel become exposed to the weather and there are several opportunities to weigh up conditions and if needs be to linger until calm returns.

Under Mike's chairmanship my friends ranged themselves on the deck like some revolutionary cabinet, and quickly became known as the Steering Committee, arguing every shift in the wind as we floated down towards Sea Reach, the last before the confluence with the Medway and the great expanse of the lower estuary. Here, having ridden the tide well enough, we were able to take the next flood into the Medway itself, and then divert into the Swale, the winding channel that separates the Isle of Sheppey from the mainland.

The Swale provides a little more shelter for those who seek it. My own first ventures in a sailing boat were made here, long ago now, but I remembered the mud vividly enough and the necessity of following the channel closely even near high water. The old anchorage at Harty Ferry still remained at the eastern end, better patronized than in the days when it supported just one solitary black schooner, for all the world like a pirate ship off the shores of Hispaniola. Nowadays a small armada resides at Harty, with the benefit of the odd untenanted buoy for passing travellers such as ourselves. Since it saved us the horrendous task of pitching overboard the mighty anchor, and all the uncertainties of choosing the right position to do

The outer harbour at Ramsgate

seven at the Varne Light Vessel, a wind strong enough to frighten the trousers off most God-fearing barge skippers but strangely at odds with the glassy calm outside. As the Varne was little more than a dozen miles away, and as the Station Report had been transmitted only an hour or so previously, a telephone call seemed in order, to clarify the problem. Soon enough we learned from the local met office that there had been a misreading, and that the man on the radio should have said 'Force one'.

We had got another calm and took it, a straightforward passage south of the Goodwins and all the way to the pier-heads of Calais. And apart from the odd lightship or marker buoy, and the occasional ferry whistling past in a flurry of seagulls, there was little to note on the way. In flat calm conditions and with the engine running at three-quarters throttle *Arthur* covered the thirty miles or so from Ramsgate in just over five hours.

As the fishermen wound in their lines from the Calais pier, and a watery sunset developed down-Channel, the Steering Committee ranged itself for a ceremonial aperitif before setting out for a victory spread on shore.

Later, when *Arthur* crossed the harbour, a man shouted from a large white motor cruiser. 'Where're you taking that?'

'Oh', someone said, 'just into the canals.'

so, we seized the largest mooring in sight, and willingly paid a few coins to the old man in a rowing boat who came out and said it was his. Lying there in comfort with the stove roaring and the evening meal prepared, we could wait in security until the next ebb began, to take us down to the Foreland and round towards Calais itself.

In the event the sea became choppy again the next day, and although not of the same worrying proportions as at Wells, it seemed wiser to seek the shelter of Ramsgate, the traditional port for waiting, before taking the plunge towards France.

Ramsgate is a friendly place for pleasure craft now-adays, although the fish and chips are indifferent. There was more forecast trouble here, the BBC listing Force

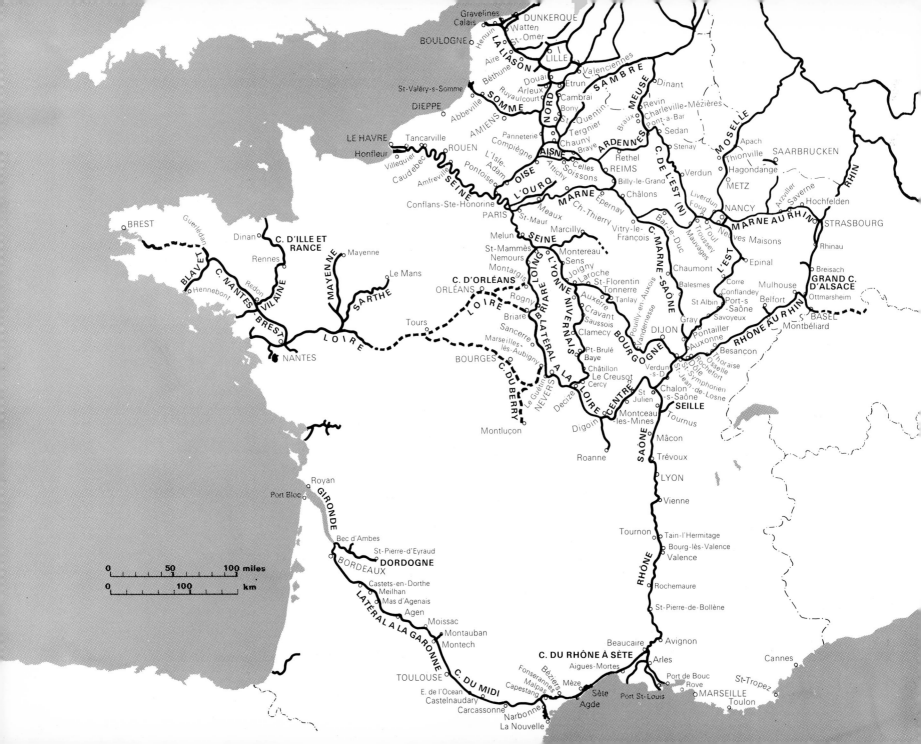

The French Canals~Introduction

The French river and canal system is a complicated one, and it is difficult to cover these waterways without twitching and weaving like a butterfly. There are many junctions, while sometimes through the accidents of history, a navigation may change its title several times. In the following pages the French waterways have been broken down into stages that may be more easily picked out by those wishing to follow. Further chapters cover stretches not travelled in *Arthur*, but visited at other times, and on these I have compared notes with other voyagers.

If I can proffer one word of advice at this point it is on the question of 'how far can I travel in one week.' Yachtsmen voyaging inland from Calais to the Mediterranean generally estimate four weeks for such a passage, while by pushing equally hard it is possible to go from Le Havre to Marseilles in three weeks. At such a pace the voyage must be purgatory, and it is little wonder that so many of these travellers discount the passage as tiresome and frustrating. It is also possible to drive a car from Calais to the Riviera and to be bored to distraction, while those who walk the smallest portion in between can instead be entranced.

It may be worth quoting *Arthur*'s schedule. In the first year we travelled on average 200km (125 miles) each week, passing through seventy locks. In fine weather and with no hold-ups this is an acceptable distance; but wherever there are delays or bad weather such progress imposes an undeniable strain. There is shopping to be done, the boat to maintain, and much more important, the sights to see and the countryside to relish. Furthermore the hours of lock opening are shorter as the season comes to its end; and here, as never before, it pays to be unambitious.

Having left the boat to winter in France, I revised my calculations. The average for *Arthur*'s second summer was 130km (80 miles) with forty locks and this is the pace I recommend, although a desire to travel more slowly still is quite understandable.

The chapters following should provide some guidance on which sections are worth lingering in. Because we went that way, and because it is a route commonly taken, I have also inserted a note on the German Moselle and Rhine.

What follows, however, is largely about France, with which, like so many, I have a love-hate relationship. I have tried to indicate the atmosphere and flavour of each portion, although this of course is as I see it. I have also incorporated as much practical information as is reasonable, short of destroying the adventure entirely.

In following a tortuous path through the system some waterways were covered more than once. In such cases experiences have been combined as of a single journey, while in the further interests of clarity I have not dwelt upon laying-up the boat for the intervening winter, although a note on leaving craft overseas is incorporated in the Appendix.

The inland waterways of France. Scale is important; Paris and Le Havre are roughly the same distance apart as Birmingham and London.

Calais

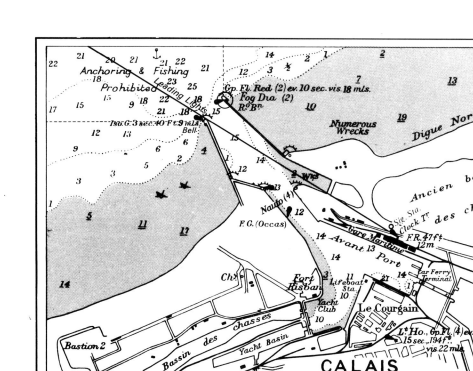

Calais harbour

French cheese and decent bread begin here, and so does many an inland voyage. The tangy aroma of a Continental harbour will be familiar to many while those who have arrived in small craft will know at first hand, quite literally, the unique grey sludge, redolent of blanc-mange, fish innards and old laundry washings, that lies so thickly on the dockside ladders.

One of the particular hazards of Calais is the heavy swell that often prevails in the outer portion of the harbour. Together with the movement of ships, the smell of drains and the natural rise and fall through the tides it can make mooring here something of an adventure. The solution is to pass through a lock into one of the non-tidal basins.

Arthur spent some time in the Bassin Ouest, where the yacht club moorings are. Here, officially, visiting craft may lie in exchange for money, but the only space remaining was not long enough for us. A place further along the wall is free, albeit beyond the sanctuary of the club compound and within the orbit of car delivery drivers, sightseers from the beach, and elderly fishermen wanting to borrow things. It is also within the exercise area of the local sailing school, which is peopled by keen athletic youths in baseball caps and very short shorts. One of their dinghies would occasionally thunder into *Arthur*'s side, an enervating experience if the Captain had drifted into a coma on the lavatory down below.

Having got to Calais earlier than expected I was left on my own for some time and so set to scraping, painting and making up various components, all in searing heat. Stocking the ship with special tools and paint before leaving England is a quite unnecessary precaution, for the French shops are nowadays well supplied, and self-service ironmongers can often be found which hold, if anything, an even wider range of goods than their equivalents in Britain. Notwithstanding I had provisioned as if for a siege and brought a range of special devices with me; few were of any use, and usually the long-standing

A confusion of cranes and gantries at the entrance to the
Bassin Carnot. The large tower on the right carries the
entrance signals.

primitive methods proved the best. Briefly I used a unique
paint removing tool, a cluster of cogwheels and flails, all
mounted in a high-speed drill, but it flew into a thousand
pieces at the moment of first application. With the memory
of its components twinkling briefly as they sank into the
harbour I passed the time away scraping by hand.

Finally came the time to move. Although the Bassin
Ouest is the recognized mooring for pleasure craft, it is
sealed by tidal doors which are opened at high Water
only. For this reason some people prefer to brave the
swells of the outer harbour to avoid the wait and to put
them nearer to the Bassin Carnot, through which the
canals are entered. There the entrance has a proper lock

which is open at both ends for a brief period, and with a
bit of low cunning it is possible to dash from one basin
to the other, from Ouest to Carnot, in the few moments in
which all gates are open simultaneously. Accordingly
I rushed through grinning like a fool, and narrowly escaped
death at the hands of the two harbour tugs *Courageux* and
Triomphant which charged out in the opposite direction.
There are red lights on a gantry that signify when entry
to the Bassin Carnot is undesirable, but in the hysteria
of high tide these are easy to overlook.

Inside the Bassin Carnot ships unload ore into the grimi-
est barges in France. Another favoured cargo is timber, in
handy propeller-sized chunks, and a lot of this is floating
around.

Entry to the French canals is free, as is their use by
private pleasure craft. Apart from towing charges at the
various tunnels and the occasional anachronistic oddity,
such as the payment for crossing the Loire at Decize, no
further levies are made. At the time of writing, however,
there is one important condition: that visiting craft remain
in the country for six months only in any one year, although
bonding under a Customs seal is permitted for the periods in
between. As an alternative to this arrangement import duty
must be paid, and at the time of my own arrival this stood
at around 29 per cent of the estimated value of the boat,
the estimation taking the form of a protracted debate in
which the owner claims his vessel to be worthless, save in
sentimental terms, while the authorities attribute a value
beyond his wildest dreams.

In order to keep tabs on all voyages a single document
was issued, the celebrated Green Card. This was an
important bit of paper, for while Customs officers might
be more or less indifferent to the whole business, the first
lock-keeper on the canal system was not, and he tended to
send people back to get one. The Green Card acted as a
passport for the 'yacht', as all pleasure craft are termed,
and it was this that had to be given up at the end of a so-
journ in France, or when the boat was placed in bond. I got
Arthur's from two Customs men found wandering near the
harbour entrance; they came back aboard to fill in the
forms and were most cordial, even when the tall one

Péniches lying empty

walked into one of our roof beams. At the far end of the Bassin Carnot, the Card was solemnly checked again by the lock-keeper there, a square-faced man obviously used to wrangling with wayward Englishmen. At that time another document, the *Permis de Circulation*, was also required; on this the intended route was listed, and although the *Permis* was free and apparently available to everyone, it had to be shown at all control points. There the facts could be entered into mighty ledgers and the *Permis* stamped, often in the wrong place, before you were allowed to proceed. All this happened at the end of the Bassin Carnot before passing through the electrically controlled lock which unexpectedly drops craft down

again and into the canal basin beyond.

Here may be found a good if somewhat dusty mooring in the shadow of the magnificent town hall, and under close scrutiny from the boat trains from Milan. French barges lie here, the traditional *péniches*, carefully moored so that no-one's cabin lies directly alongside another. *Arthur* stayed through Independence Day, when the canals are closed, and all around boat people were proudly hoisting tricolours to the accompaniment of *Marseillaise*-type noises from the town. From time to time children from the *péniches* would come scurrying by, always cheerful and talking in clear, simple French. A tiny child in a headscarf and carrying a shopping bag would stop for ages asking about the boat, and where we had come from. Would she look after *Arthur* while I went off on the bike to meet my friends? Yes, but there would be no need. No one ever touched anything when there were *péniches* about. And indeed that is true; when you moor among such craft you moor in a tiny community, in which all the niceties are observed and every courtesy shown but little goes unremarked. It is like being in a small country town or village.

A good bicycle on a boat saves hours, and with one it is possible to whizz around the Calais shops in a fraction of the time that it takes to walk. No road user gives way to any other in France, save to traffic approaching from the right — a weird and disastrous rule which implies that Grand Prix racers should yield to horse-drawn carts emerging through a gap in the hedge. And so, even now that priority routes have been ordained, a good set of gears is necessary on a bike, to allow a quick getaway at ambiguous intersections. A bicycle also makes a splendid pack mule for the mountainous stacks of luggage that new crews bring.

Having met my first crew safely, and set a one week course to Tergnier, a railway junction in the fields south of St-Quentin, I reflected that Calais had not been such a bad spot after all. A lot of jokes are made about it, but it has good shops and eating houses in the old town about a mile inland from the port, and a pleasant minor resort of the Monsieur Hulot variety just over the sand dunes to seaward of the Bassin Ouest. There are far worse places to stay.

Children from the boats (*Albert Barber*)

The railway passes close at hand

Canal de Calais and the River Aa

Calais to Watten, 36km (20 miles) and 1 lock

The canal from Calais is a minor one by French standards, cutting in straight tacks across flat countryside. It is entered by turning left after the Bassin Carnot. Several lift bridges follow, manned with understandable torpor by gentlemen in concrete kiosks. Here a powerful hooter is a great asset. The *péniches* have thunderous klaxons of many decibels and do not hesitate to use them; nor do lock or bridge-keepers generally take offence, for a blaring horn does not have the same connotations of anger as in England. The average yacht hooter is in fact no good, being far too gentle and discreet; what is needed is the sort of noise that will negotiate a double bend beneath an autoroute and penetrate the plate glass windows of a vessel coming the other way, for ideally the hooter must perform this function as well.

Overtaking. Here the *péniche* has moved well over, but passing would have been difficult and ill-advised at the bend in the background.

There are not many bends on the Canal de Calais, but it is an attractive waterway all the same, running through wide fields, alternately black and green and with the traditional border of lofty trees. Anyone wishing to sample the essence of the French canals can do far worse than to enter the Canal de Calais and to journey along it just as far as the next lock which is fifteen miles inland. It may be added that for those in haste and heading south, this is the only really bucolic section until well beyond Paris, for the rest of that route lies along major arteries, with concrete banks, space-age control cabins, and less of the olde worlde.

If there is one thing that will slow the traveller down, however, it is overhauling a loaded *péniche*, for there is a strict *politesse* in such matters, and a loaded boat in an old canal has to pick her way along slowly. Whether a 'yacht' can overtake depends upon the lie of the land, the goodwill of the steerer ahead, and also upon the distance to the next lock.

We caught up with our first *péniche* labouring heavily through a narrow section at about two knots, the steerer's arm seen in silhouette through the rear wheelhouse window and the huge wheel spinning this way and that as the vessel drove forward through clouds of mud. In such circumstances it is essential etiquette to wait astern until the *péniche* can move aside and a hand appears in invitation to pass. It is then up to the overtaker to push by and to clear the next lock with a minimum of delay.

The whereabouts of all locks and bridges are clearly shown in a series of strip maps, published in the *Guide de la Navigation Intérieure* (see Appendix). With this on the cabin top it is possible to see ahead a little and to know, for instance, whether overtaking is desirable.

The next lock was at the hamlet of Henuin, and it is the only one on the Canal de Calais, or the short section of the River Aa that follows. At Henuin we found all the elements: some wriggling bends, a dignified blue-denimed keeper, a cafe, and an ancient moored vessel, the *Rien sans Dieu*, providing support for slumbering anglers. As is customary at all hand-wound locks we worked the equipment with the keeper, and told him of the *péniche* we had passed, since getting the lock ready was his responsibility. The French do not generally 'lock wheel', as in England, and anyone dashing ahead to lend a hand is regarded as something of a phenomenon.

The area left lasting impressions, of beaming *madame* at the cafe, of the *péniche* we had overtaken being steered into the lock without a touch, although we ourselves had clouted the abutment quite severely. This is an impressionistic area. I remember the closeness of the trees when we set off again on the following morning, the last swing bridge in a position of absolute peace, and the final tree-enshrouded junction with the River Aa.

The local scene. It behoves the voyager to slip by quietly and without wash (*Albert Barber*).

The Aa runs into the sea at Gravelines and the canal system can also be entered from there, although only at high tide and when the weather is not too fierce. However, the Canal de Calais joins the river in an upstream reach and this is tideless. By turning back towards the coast the traveller can light upon another rural waterway, the Canal de Bourbourg, which gives access to Dunkerque and ultimately to Belgium. But the majority of visitors turn inland instead, towards a new industrial canal, the Liason Dunkerque-Valenciennes, that sweeps directly across the northwest corner of France.

Craft entering the canal system at Dunkerque do so through a maze of docks somewhat similar to those at Calais. There is a choice of locks, but the smallest, l'Ecluse Tristram, is perhaps the most advisable in this busy harbour. To join the Liason it is necessary to thread back towards the Bassin Maritime, just within the sea wall, for it is here that this new canal enters the port.

La Liason Dunkerque~ Valenciennes

Watten to Etrun, 123km (76 miles) and 6 locks

The Liason is really a chain of waterways, sometimes listed separately as the Canal d'Aire, Canal de la Deule, and so on. It has been modernized to take trains of barges, grouped together and pushed by a single tug, but the bulk of the craft *Arthur* encountered were 350-ton *péniches*.

The Liason: wide, straight and busy

Locks near Douai are electrically controlled. *Arthur* passes through with a single *péniche*, but a further six were descending at the same time in another chamber alongside.

After the little canal from Calais, this huge motorway-like dyke comes as something of a shock. It even has no-entry symbols at triangular junctions and '*Garage*' at places deemed safe to moor. These are indeed the only sheltered places, save near the occasional locks or down old arms at townships such as St-Omer and Aire, for the banks are harshly concreted and the traffic vigourous. No longer do the *péniches* drag along over the shoals; instead they pound forward and the wash that they make is formidable.

In the course of modernization, several old loops have been bypassed, and as these are often now blocked they tend to serve as moorings for barge people in retirement, awaiting birth, or sometimes just taking a break, lying alongside the craft of relatives and friends. It is often difficult to pick a way through such a congregation (although advice is freely given, for any craft actually on the move attracts attention). The net result is that it is awkward to reach the centre of any large town, save by bicycle or a very long walk. There is a short sheltered arm near Aire, where there is a pleasant and cheerful square beyond the battered church; and the remnants of an old loop outside Béthune (a two mile walk). But frequently the disorganized voyager is obliged to moor to the kerb of the main line itself. In addition to the *Guide*, which along this route follows the old route of the canal, I have found large scale Michelin maps quite invaluable. With their help it is often possible to stop near a village which might otherwise be concealed over the canal bank.

If stopping on the main line it is necessary to put out many tyres and ropes. For a boat of *Arthur*'s size mooring spikes have proved useless, as they invariably tweak out as soon as the first vessel gallops past. We would therefore look for bollards or rings, which often lie buried in the long grass, and since these are rarely less than a *péniche*-length apart, we usually moored *Arthur* bow and stern to the same one, using the engine to pin him in really tight.

There are few locks on the Liason but those that exist are cavernous and electrically operated. Each can hold many craft, and although it is sometimes wise to let barges enter first it is equally advisable not to be browbeaten and thus excluded from a lock altogether. Sometimes locks are arranged in pairs, but while this may halve the waiting time there is usually double the traffic, so once again it is necessary to insist upon taking one's turn. This is what all the other captains expect anyway.

Once the fleet has been entombed in a lock a loudspeaker commands anyone who has not done so to clamber up to the control tower and to deliver his *papiers* to the keeper. After blundering into several empty rooms and cabinets full of switchgear, I discovered that one is meant to put the *Permis*, or failing that the 'ship's papers', into one of those pipe systems operated by air pressure. There follows a stilted conversation through the intercom, and it

The lift of Les Fontinettes near St-Omer, opened in 1887 and recently replaced by a modern lock. Craft were raised or lowered through 43ft in two counterbalanced caissons.

helps to know the French pronunciation of the letters of the alphabet that comprise your name. What the keeper is really listening for, however, is the clink of a coin in a strategically placed jam-jar. The cross-examination then ceases. Contrary to a popular British belief, tipping is not generally necessary on the hand-wound locks of France, nor do many keepers expect it. *Péniche* crews often leave a coin of payola, but only the technocrats at these huge modern locks seem to require baksheesh as of right. Since the demise of the *Permis* such habits still persist, and it is therefore useful to have 'papers' of some sort or another,

in order to go through such formalities without embarass-ment.

Near St-Omer stands the old lift of Fontinettes, opened in 1887 and a very close relative of the only British canal lift still working, that at Anderton in Cheshire. The Fonti-nettes lift raised and lowered craft a distance of 43ft in counterbalanced caissons – until 1967 when a replace-ment lock was opened. At that moment someone must have blown a whistle, for the old workshops alongside appear to have been abandoned as if in fright. Tools have been downed in mid-task, or so it appears, and at the time of my own visit the dust-covered machines still stood in Marie-Celestian splendour. It was also possible to clamber all over the lift itself, for only the most half-hearted dis-mantling had taken place.

Traffic on the Liason congregates in such areas as Douai, in jam-packed moorings near the steelworks and factories, where the atmosphere is identically that of the Birmingham canals twenty-five or thirty years ago. This alone invests these northern canals with a certain fascina-tion, while such industrial squalor as exists is more re-stricted than in England.

To visit such a village as Fressies, not far from where the Canal du Nord branches off towards Paris, is to be reassured that agricultural France remains as ever. Horse-flies, wasps and mosquitos abound too, incidentally, and while these are a nuisance, and particularly in the evening when the choice lies between suffocation and being eaten alive, there are many consolations. The canalsides of France swarm with butterflies, dragonflies and wild flowers, for toxic sprays are not widely used, while at night, once the insects have gone to bed, it is possible to experience total silence and to look around an horizon un-marked by any light.

Navigationally this part of the system offers interest in its steady traffic, and also in the floating dredgers, which suck mud from the bottom and by means of floating pipes blast it into the fields alongside at a rate that would clear the English canals in a matter of hours. It is advisable to proceed cautiously at such points and to look for any signals or frantic gesticulation which might mean there are moor-

Typical double lock, near Cambrai. A British motor boat
heads for Calais.

Cast iron lock-keeper's cabin, now replaced
by a concrete tower. Buildings of this type still
endure on the Canal de St-Quentin.

Canal de St~Quentin

104km (65 miles) and 40 locks, including l'Escaut from Etrun to Cambrai

ing lines across the canal. If there are, it appears to be the custom to hoot thunderously, and then press on regardless, but the visitor is wise to wait until the way is cleared. As a waterway to steer along it must be admitted that the Liason is not very demanding.

Arthur entered this leg through a short section of the Escaut, allegedly the top of the Schelde, but in this portion really an old-time canal. After the Liason it was like turning back the pages. A gnome-like lock-keeper made a great fuss about which bollards we should moor to in the chamber, and also about any photos that might be taken, these apparently being forbidden. I suspected that he had suffered in times past as a touristic curiosity, and so could not blame him. Finally he appeared with what looked like a little whip with a clothes peg on it, and this he lowered down for the inevitable *papiers*. He stamped the *Permis* with great deliberation and force, the stamp unfortunately not really working.

Entering the tunnel at Bony, over three miles long. Loaded boats go first, empties next, yachts last of all. *Arthur* was seventeenth in the line. Total time to pass through two tunnels and an intermediate cutting in which tows cross is eight hours. Both tunnels are electrically lit.

All the locks on this route are doubled, that is with two chambers side by side, each electrified by a gimcrack arrangement of motors and chains, but all working smoothly under control from the cast iron cabins.

The big event on the Canal de St-Quentin is the passage through the tunnels of Bony, 5670m long, and Lesdins, 1098m. Craft are towed through both, and along the narrow winding section in the deep countryside in between. The prime object of the towing is to prevent asphyxiation from diesel fumes and electric tugs are used,

looking like a cross between Nelson's *Victory* and a Wild West saloon. Each tug hauls itself along a chain laid on the bed of the canal, and the power is taken from overhead wires, beneath which the boat people stroll unconcernedly on their craft tethered in line astern.

There are two departures a day in each direction, the journey lasting eight hours and the tows crossing in a deep cutting at the southern end of Bony. Precisely what the starting times are is difficult to ascertain, as each source of reference says something different, while none of the lock-keepers on the ascent from Cambrai are any better informed. As the years go by the departures subtly vary. Suffice to say there is one tow in the morning and another in the evening.

A charge is levied at the top lock and from this there is no escape as the rules compel all craft to pay; *Arthur* cost 51.66 francs. A certain amount of shunting also takes place, loaded *péniches* going to the front of the train (or *râme*), empties next, and any 'yacht' last of all, hanging by a single rope from the offside bollard of the vessel in front.

Inside the tunnels the *péniche* families go below to eat, and indeed there is little point in steering, although a stout bough jammed between the bitts of a bollard is a good wrinkle for keeping off the wall. *Arthur* lay astern of the *Diapason* of Cambrai, which played its transistor. Towing speed was about $1\frac{1}{2}$ knots, and over the years crews have enlivened the passage by painting names on the walls. John Alexander was there in 1962. There is also neon lighting from time to time, a rubbish strewn towpath, and on that side a wooden rubbing strip so worn that it has become recessed.

In the open air section the tow tends to grind around the bends but, this apart, gliding along here is quite a 'Cider With Rosie' experience. An emerging *râme* also seems to be something of a tourist attraction, for despite completion of the parallel Canal du Nord in 1965, traffic on the St-Quentin has remained fairly constant. There were sixteen *péniches* in our *râme* (the record being said to be seventy-four).

The tunnels on the St-Quentin are representative

Electric tunnel tugs at Bony. A heavy chain is picked up from the canal bed and fed over pulleys, while power is drawn from overhead wires.

of the straightening and improvement that took place on many parts of the system during the second half of the nineteenth century. Whereas in England many canals were under pressure from the railway companies and already in decline, on the Continent waterways were protected and expanded. The Freycinet Act, passed in 1879, was fundamental to their future. This provided for a general reconstruction to a common standard, that of the *péniche* still so widely seen today, measuring 38.5m in length, 5.05m in beam (with locks of 5.20m) and a loaded depth of 2m. If hereafter 'Freycinet waterways' are referred to, it is to those that accommodate craft of such a size.

At the end of a tow there's a great sort-out, everyone having discreetly noted the order in which they first arrived. Because of the double lock system, however, there are few delays, and the canal is deep enough for the more powerful loaded craft to bomb along at a fast bicycling speed. Furthermore the locks have been widened slightly, which obviates the customary painful struggle to leave, for when *péniches* are a dead fit they have to work hard to displace the water within a lock chamber. We saw one motor yacht, behaving very badly, pass a *péniche* waiting for a lock. The *péniche* captain merely took it back by motoring hard to indicate that all ahead must get out of the way. At which the yacht did so, just.

The canal passes through World War territory, and there is ample evidence of this in the many graveyards and memorials. Elsewhere corn sprouts where once men died, and although it is difficult even now to put such thoughts aside, I found the countryside much more attractive than I had been led to believe. Only at the southern end, where the surroundings are marshy and where stands Tergnier, the French Crewe, can it be said to be doleful.

The towns, such as St-Quentin itself, mix ancient history, echoes of the more recent fighting (in the shape of badly damaged churches), and the marked sophistication of present-day urban France.

The Canal de St-Quentin, near the summit

Speaking French

At such a point, after a week or so of travelling, the average Briton is beginning to relax a bit and perhaps even essaying a few chosen *bon mots* with thunderstruck lock-keepers. Fluency in French undoubtedly increases one's relish of the country. It materializes, in my own experience, with drunkenness or with anger (and to this end an excellent place to practice is that part of the Bassin Ouest in Calais at which speedboat drivers roar up and down to check their engines).

In short, confidence is an important asset in speaking. But this does not seem to be all; as an indifferent linguist myself, I have nonetheless studied the problem and come to the following conclusions, here listed in the hope they will be of value to others in this familiar predicament.

To French ears English is an incredibly harsh and jarring language. It is for this reason that Britons are so often taken for German, even when trying to speak French. French is an ultra-soft language, and it seems much more important to speak it so than to get the grammar right; such at any rate is my own experience. I wish someone had told me this at school.

'Please' and 'if you please' are very important terms. From experience I have learned that *S'il vous plaît Monsieur*, or *Madame*, goes a long way at the lockside, in the restaurant, or when out buying. *Avez-vous*, literally 'have you?' is disastrous by comparison with *Est-ce que vous avez?* and often makes the difference between getting something, such as drinking water, use of a hose, or dinner, and not getting it at all. If a Frenchman thinks you are German into the bargain, and if he is one of the several who do not like Germans, then what he takes as rudeness only confirms him in his hatreds. Some Frenchmen don't like English people either, but I would rather be hated for what I am than for what I am not. While still on this delicate subject it might be added that many French lock-keepers do not recognise a Union Jack when they see it; neither do they always know or care where Southampton is, or for that matter London. So what you hang or write on your boat does not always explain your nationality.

The reaction of a French lock-keeper, angler, or hotelier to a British boat crew arriving on his patch corresponds exactly to the reverse situation in England. I don't know if this has a direct practical bearing, but find it a useful reflection in times of international tension.

Northern entrance to the Souterrain de la Panneterie.

Canal du Nord

95km (59 miles) and 19 locks

Another modern canal, the Nord provides the quickest inland route towards Paris from Calais and Dunkerque. It is extensively used by barge traffic, with modern locks and other works, albeit on not quite the same scale as the Liason Dunkerque-Valenciennes. It has an intriguing history, in that by the onset of World War I its construction was over half completed, but all this work was destroyed in the subsequent fighting. The canal was finally opened in 1965.

The locks are electrically operated and there are also two tunnels along the course. The longest of these, the 4350m Souterrain de Ruyaulcourt, has single line working, but craft can enter from each end simultaneously, passing in the central section of the tunnel, which has been widened for this purpose. Fortunately the system is controlled by traffic lights, and two people I met travelling in a tiny 15ft sailing dinghy told me that although they had entered in great trepidation, their passage had not been unobserved, and a convoy of *péniches* waited in the middle to let them pass. This tunnel is in the northern portion. The other, the 1100m Souterrain de la Panneterie, is to the south, and here lights control a more conventional single line system, craft working, as before, under their own power.

The old line of the Canal de la Somme is partially incorporated into the Nord, and this trails off eastward in its old-fashioned way to form an additional link with the Canal de St-Quentin. The Canal de la Somme also diverges towards the sea, leaving the Canal du Nord at a point 45km and twelve locks from its northern end.

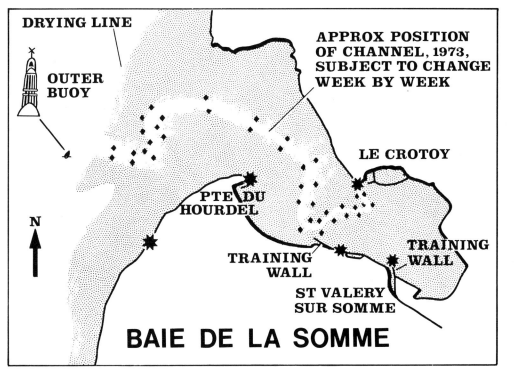

DRYING LINE

OUTER BUOY

APPROX POSITION
OF CHANNEL, 1973,
SUBJECT TO CHANGE
WEEK BY WEEK

LE CROTOY

N

PTE DU
HOURDEL

TRAINING
WALL

TRAINING
WALL

ST VALERY
SUR SOMME

BAIE DE LA SOMME

Courtesy of *Practical Boat Owner*.

Canal de la Somme

119km (74 miles) and 19 locks between
Biaches (junction with the Nord) and the sea

The Somme navigation, part river, part canal, winds for
the most part through an area of gravel pits and marshland, calling at nowhere in particular, save the city of
Amiens and the township of Abbeville. Both were heavily
involved in the two world wars, and largely knocked to
pieces in the second. There is a not unattractive lone-
someness about the surrounding region, with soaring trees
often picking out the line of the waterway among the
pools and scrubland in the vicinity.

Occasional locks lie between the Nord and the sea, and
these are elderly hand-winders, with assistance from
keepers who are often startled to find any traffic at all.
In the course of several visits to the section between
Amiens and Abbeville I have only once seen a *péniche*
on the move.

Eastward of Abbeville the canal runs dead straight,
joining the estuary through a sea lock to the southeast of
St-Valery-sur-Somme, where there is a short sheltered
creek. The Somme estuary itself is extremely shallow, with
all the normal dangers of such regions. Those navigating
must wait for settled weather and high water for the
channels are marked somewhat haphazardly by buoys and
beacons. Crews entering from seaward are well advised
to make first for Boulogne or Dieppe and there take stock
and perhaps acquire local charts, for navigation in such
strange and shallow waters can only be undertaken in the
calmest conditions. Nor is it for the inexperienced.

Braye Tunnel, the Tête Aisne

Electric mule of the type once widespread on the towpaths
of northern France

From Chauny to
Berry~au~Bac

71km (44 miles) and 14 locks

A chain of waterways provides a short cut from the
southern end of the St-Quentin for vessels heading east.
The first of these is the Canal de l'Oise a l'Aisne, entered
just beyond a rare but traditionally decrepit canalside
yard at Chauny. For the first part the Oise a l'Aisne passes

through marshland, but climbs gradually to a tunnel of
2365m at Braye-en-Laonnois.

Arthur lay for the night here astern of a vessel called
Satie, skippered by an amiable and generous spirited
individual lightly covered in part of his cargo, which
happened to be coal. His many children eyed us with
apparent interest but proved to be awaiting the erection
of the ubiquitous television aerial. TV has all but killed
social life on the French canals, and most of the inns are
now closed. All that remain are a few painted signs, nowadays badly faded, saying *Auberge de la Marine, Cafe du
Port*, and so on. Such is the pressure of work today that the
barge people slog on until the locks close for the night and
they can go no further. Then, poised for an early start the
following day, usually before 6.30am, and preferably
in such a position that no-one can steal past in the meantime, they put up their aerials and go below.

The tunnel entrances at Braye are impressively known
as Tête Oise and Tête Aisne. Tête Oise is tree-enshrouded
and quite sinister in the streaming rain. Had we known
better we could have stopped beforehand just above the
summit lock where there is a convenient wharf, and
dinghy sailing to look at on an attractive lake alongside.
It had been a mistake to follow the *péniche*, for the mooring points outside tunnels are almost invariably non-
places, strewn with old rubbish and waste engine oil, put
there by those who service their motors while waiting.
Bins are sometimes provided, both for rubbish and for
the oil, but do not always appear to be emptied.

At 6.30 in the morning *Arthur* was towed through
behind the *Satie* and the immaculate *Dino* from Belgium.
This time the towing was by small motors suspended from
a rail beneath the roof, escorted by an elderly gentleman
stumbling through the cataracts and puddles of the towpath. Future travellers have been spared this depressing
spectacle, for a large ventilation fan has since been
installed at the Tête Aisne to permit craft to go through
under their own power.

The locks on the Oise a l'Aisne are electric, and most
courteously manned, often by middle aged ex-soldiers.
This area is another within the orbit of intensive fighting,

A long hose permits a boat to continue working through a
lock while refilling.

The Canal Latéral a l'Aisne which follows is once again
in the swamps, at least as far as Berry-au-Bac, where there
is a turn-off for Reims. There are signs on the way of the
old towing system whereby craft were once pulled by
small electric locomotives or 'mules', which jolted along
an uneven track, drawing their current from overhead
wires. When one mule met another they merely exchanged
towlines and set off back the way they had come, so that
it was possible for a driver to spend his entire working day
running a shuttle service a couple of hundred yards long.
Until 1939 some eighty or ninety per cent of French
barges were either propelled in this way or drawn by real
mules, and the system persisted until 1968 when government subsidies came to an end and the traction companies
closed. Electric mules remain at certain tunnels where
they act as tugs, but elsewhere there are only twisted rails
and the occasional posts for the power lines. At Bourg-et-
Comin, a lonely junction in the middle of nowhere, I
found a small shack containing remnants of the old control
system: some telephones and a blackboard upon which
the whereabouts of various locos had been noted.

Drinking Water

At the lock at Guny on the Oise a l'Aisne we found a water
point, a fairly typical installation, where the friendly
keeper had provided a hose. Various old propellers,
brightly painted and on display, demonstrated a bond with
the boat people (a bond not all keepers share, particularly
when the hours of lock opening are in dispute). Here
captains would stop to fill up their tanks and to exchange
a word or two of gossip before forging on again.

Water points are to be found occasionally on each canal,
say once or twice a day, and at these a hose is often provided.
Those who, like ourselves, carry their own hoses will
learn from experience that they should have brought an
extremely long one, for a reach of 20m is not uncommon.
Continental tap fittings are also different from those in
Britain.

and the site of the Big Bertha cannon that shelled the
Allied armies during World War I is but a short cycle ride
to the north by the village of Coney.

Unlike the locks of the St-Quentin, which can be
fierce and which most definitely need ropes during the
ascent, these proved gentle in the extreme. As an added
curiosity those on the far side, beyond the Tête Aisne,
are theoretically automatic in operation, one of several
such types under trial in France. By passing in front of
electronic eyes and by brushing against various pads in
the walls, our boat should have set and worked the locks
on their own. Unhappily *Arthur* was not quite wide
enough to do so and had to be accompanied by another oil-
skinned officer who poked and pulled at these devices with
a walking stick.

Before leaving England I was presented with a large bottle of chemical powder for adding to drinking water whenever we thought the local supply to be suspect. Perhaps fortunately I have never used it. Old myths die hard, and it may be reassuring to léarn that French schoolchildren are warned of the local water whenever they visit Great Britain. Certainly I have never found bad water on the French canals, save once when it was contaminated with plastic from a lock-keeper's hose. It is always sensible to run the tap for a while first.

It is also a good plan to carry a jerry can full of water. This can also be used at unsung water points, for all lock cottages have a supply somewhere which can provide a few gallons as a stopgap. Since filling the can often involves entering a keeper's private domain, a persuasive manner and a dog-resistant temperament are decided assets.

A useful if tyrannical means of saving water is to have only one tap on board, and it should be of a type that is not too easy to work. Such is the system on *Arthur*, where water is raised by a little hand-pump, and no-one uses more than they need. For clothes and hair washing we often use canal and river water, collecting it from the engine cooling system, which heats it up nicely. By such means the 20 gallon fresh water tank, which is small by many standards, will last eight people over a day, and often two days. Luxury yachts often have much more; but since they have pressure or electric taps that run until turned off, they probably need it. A tap that can be left running is a menace in any boat.

The matter of collecting water brings us neatly to the question of tipping, for it is at such moments that gratuities may be appropriate. Some hire boat companies in France urge their clients to tip every lock-keeper, which is not only setting a dubious precedent, but at one franc a time, as recommended, becomes ruinously expensive. I tip rarely myself, having noticed that the nicest canal servants are embarrassed by it; and if the others are not so nice, why should they be tipped anyway? The keepers on the Dunkerque-Valenciennes route use blackmail, as

explained, but few others are so mercenary. Normally I give a franc for water, at a checkpoint for papers, or where some special service has been rendered.

I have seen recommendations to offer drinks, and more particularly sweets to a lock-keeper's children, but pride can easily be offended, and the huge hairy lock-keeper I saw thrown a packet of Smarties by the crew of an English motor yacht took great delight in letting in the water before they had got any ropes ashore. From my own observation a willingness to share in the work plus some attempt at communication, however basic, is much more appreciated.

Canal des Ardennes

106km (72 miles) and 46 locks, including Latéral a l'Aisne east of Berry-au-Bac

Although the first ten miles beyond Berry-au-Bac are still technically the Canal Latéral a l'Aisne, in spirit they are part of the Canal des Ardennes which follows, and there is only a change in the name in the reference books to mark the connection between the two. Neither actually goes through the Ardennes range which spreads away from the southernmost corner of Belgium, but they do point vaguely at it.

This is a beautiful route, beginning in pine woods which gradually yield to rolling pastoral downland as the canal winds up the hillside in a final flight of twenty-seven locks. On the way lies Rethel, a much rebuilt town through which many intruders have passed. A plaque on the bridge over the Aisne commemorates successive invasions, to which someone had added in aerosol paint '1972 – La Pollution'. Unhappily this is so, and the Aisne is dirty.

Elsewhere on the western end of the canal are grain silos provided by farmers' cooperatives. Here the *péniches* are compelled to load in midstream, by means of a long

Working through the long flight from the summit of the
Canal des Ardennes, down towards Berry-au-Bac and the
junction for Reims.

working the locks, the family crew will occupy themselves
in painting the boat or in brushing away nonexistent dirt.
Carpet slippers or overshoes are often worn to prevent
scraping the deck and anyone invited aboard – a gesture
not lightly given – will be expected to remove their shoes
before going below.

Swabbing the deck – a continuous process.
Many boat people wear soft shoes in order not
to scratch the plates.

pipe from the silo top, for this is one of the shallower
waterways, down which loaded boats tack like clipper
ships as they lurch between the reefs.

Péniches vary; the odd one is scruffy, but the majority are
as smart as soldiers on parade, generally with bows and
superstructure in a rich chocolate or brown. The name of a
péniche is often devised from the names of the husband
and wife who share ownership; or sometimes of brothers,
with occasionally just initial letters instead. All craft bear
a registration number with a coded prefix, such as LI-Lille
or NY-Nancy. In between steering, cooking, washing and

Running empty

taken in turn after signing on, and waiting – the riskiest part of the business – at one of the co-operative exchanges based at the more important canal centres. Although some craft work on regular runs, many more are on a tramping system, travelling widely from country to country, wherever the next load may take them.

These vessels, though often attractive, are practical in the extreme. The propeller for instance is mounted on the waterline when the *péniche* is empty, being enclosed within a metal tunnel to prevent it flailing the air, but accessible by means of removable panels. A steering wheel or propeller casing hanging outside the wheelhouse of a moored craft is a symbol that such water level work is being carried out. Similarly a red flag on display will indicate a breakdown or other vulnerability, and it requests that craft passing should do so slowly and without wash.

Years ago I saw Jean Vigo's film *L'Atalante*, which is set on a *péniche* of that name, and watched the crew swing themselves on and off the ship by means of a pivoting derrick. I thought it a gimmick at the time, but have since seen dozens of boat people set themselves ashore by this method, kicking themselves from the deck and apparently hanging in mid-air as the long spar swings them towards some bank that loaded craft cannot easily reach. Many *péniches* now also carry cars, usually on the hatches or stern deck, and these are driven off by means of planks and careful adjustment of the levels when a boat is in a lock.

In keeping with all this, the *péniches* are handled with a care and precision very much at odds with the lackadaisical mannerisms of English bargemen. Every *péniche* entering a lock is steered all the way in. There is no question of scraping the sides; indeed I have seen a boatman going over his rubbing strips with a scrubbing brush.

The people of the barges, the *batellerie*, are reasonably prosperous and, although trade has had its ups and downs, receive good money when working. Many cargoes are international, a load of grain, the commonest commodity, taking perhaps two weeks to transport from the Yonne, or Seine Basin, to Belgium or to the Netherlands. Loads are

The long flight of locks towards the summit of the Canal des Ardennes is untypical of the French canals as a whole, for generally locks are evenly distributed, and there is some opportunity of overtaking. When locks are closely spaced, as here, speed is dictated by the closeness of the boat in front, and although empty *péniches* career along the cut like carpet sweepers in fully cry, loaded craft move slowly in such shallow waters and have to struggle hard to enter and leave the locks. Far from bombing out in a shower of sparks and imprecations, as the English narrow boat was wont to do, a French *péniche* sits stolidly in the lock like Pooh Bear, thinking things over. Closer examination will reveal that in fact that engine is running quite hard, but with over 350 tons to shift and with a lot of water to squeeze through the tiny gap on each side, a loaded boat accelerates imperceptibly. Likewise when two craft meet in a narrow waterway they will stay locked like dinosaurs in combat. Engines thunder, the water boils, but passing can take an age; and so can waiting astern of it all, although the scene is not without some compensatory drama. Despite all this the *péniches* have a hare and tortoise knack of covering the ground, surviving on their itch to keep moving. At about twenty minutes a lock they can climb the twenty-seven in nine or ten hours, or roughly three-quarters of the working day.

The atmosphere on this final flight is remarkably English, and the countryside has the quality of a child's picture book. The lock-keepers here tend to be stoical rather than sprightly and when not stacking wood in anticipation of the winter to end all winters, they have turned to other pursuits, such as raising chickens or breeding rabbits, which occupy rambling tenements by the canalside.

After the summit level there is a short descent to the River Meuse, enlivened for us by the sight of an otter swimming with a baby otter in its mouth, and for travellers in general by the tunnel of St-Aignan, which has a sharp approach. It is fortunately short enough to see through and there is just space at either end in which to retreat should the tunnel prove to be occupied.

The final connection with the river is at Pont-à-Bar, a lonesome hamlet somewhat distant in spirit from the charms before — or of the glories of the Meuse just a few miles further to the north.

The Meuse from Pont-à-Bar to Revin

57km (35 miles) and 9 locks

The River Meuse flows northwards into and through Belgium, but that portion in France is incorporated into the Canal de l'Est (branche Nord). Its most splendid reaches extend northward of the twin towns of Charleville and Mézières and these are quickly reached from Pont-à-Bar. Some gravel pits and the world's biggest gathering of electricity pylons precede the penetration of Charleville by means of two sheer and winding cuttings through the rock. One of these is sensibly controlled by traffic lights, but Mézières lock has a completely blind bend at its downstream end, and the air is frequently rent by engines howling hard astern.

Charleville's waterside is a disappointing shambles, distinguished only by a pull-in for fuel, plus some remarkable graffiti. It is the custom of the boat people to chalk messages, often on lock gates or on the beams beneath

Local children from Deville, a small village in the woods near the Belgian border

On the Meuse north of Charleville

Boating graffiti, recording names, destinations
and home ports. Dates sometimes go back to
before the war.

bridges, noting their destinations and the times of passing.
Similarly at a journey's end it is common for the younger
members of the crew to paint the vessel's name. The
wharves of Charleville are covered in such inscriptions, in
one case so thickly that there are names written over
names, and with dates going back over decades. The
earliest I saw dated back to 1931.

It is not possible to moor near the arcaded Place Ducale,
which is the town's best feature, nor particularly close to
shops, and so Charleville is remembered as one of those
places where one cannot lie properly, save among concrete
ruins or at the rat-infested bank by the fuel jetty. The
long traipse into the town confirms these earlier sour
impressions. It seems to be one of those places where it is
either raining, has recently rained, or is just about to,

and indeed the whole Meuse valley has a record of extended downpours.

But the wooded gorges north of Charleville revive the spirits entirely. Each reach seems more noble than the last. Green hillsides tower above the river as it twists back upon itself, at times briefly flowing south before turning yet again towards Belgium. These are the Ardennes, and in the occasional small township the *sanglier*, the wild boar symbol of the region, is prominently displayed, usually advertising beer. Strangely the villages in this French portion of the valley are poor, being often mere quarry settlements, a group of terraced houses dumped among the woods, whereas in Belgium the Meuse tends towards chalets and elegant waterfronts as at Dinant. The difference is that Dinant is in the *south* of Belgium, and the people of both countries have a higher regard for the south than for the north.

Arthur journeyed as far downstream as Revin, 40km short of the border. There are numerous lock cuts on the way, many of them perilously near to weirs, and to judge by the flood marks navigation must sometimes be an adventure. When the river is in spate the locks are often closed and the traffic controlled so as to avoid dramatic confrontations in the current. My own memories are of placid waters, although when *Arthur*'s engine unexpectedly boiled at the entrance to one of the cuts, the weir-keeper materialized like a genie to take a hastily thrown line and drag us clear of the track of a downcoming Belgian.

At the little town of Revin, a loop of the Meuse is bypassed by a short tunnel beneath the hill. Here the knowledgeable are expected to reach to one side and tug a grimy and unlabelled piece of rope hanging against the wall. This operates a bell in the lock-keeper's cabin beyond the sharp bend at the farther end, and with luck he will have set the necessary wheels in motion by the time you arrive. Those more interested in observing the ancient flood marks, one of which is a mere two feet from the roof of the tunnel, will fail to notice the rope altogether. This happened to us, and we found the keeper in a state of deep trance and the lock totally unprepared.

One further incident marked the passage. While lying in a spectacular reach near Braux we ensnared a car in our ropes. Towpaths are forbidden to the public, but like most French prohibitions this is widely ignored, and as a result somersaulting scooterists and garroted fishermen are a commonplace. As on the other hand it is also forbidden to obstruct the towpath, or to tie to trees, or to moor within a certain distance of locks, the situation if often ambiguous. Rather than argue the point, as here, before one belligerent driver wobbled away down the path, it is safer to lay obstructing lines flat on the ground. This can sometimes be done by passing them from the far side of the boat and under the hull, an old boatman's trick to which *Arthur* is well suited.

Working Locks

The Meuse affords a useful example of lock operation, for here are the two basic types, those worked by hand, and those that have been selected for electrification, apparently arbitrarily, and are worked by push-buttons from a cabin. Both types are under the control of a keeper, a variable quantity ranging widely in age, sex and outlook, and often an amateur shopkeeper and market gardener as well.

At the hand-winders the lock-keepers appreciate help from the crew, although the chamber is customarily prepared before a boat's arrival by the keeper alone. Once a lock is ready the descent is easy, and the water rarely turbulent. Someone from the crew will help to close the upper gates, and then wind some of the sluices, known as *vannes*, at the opposite end in order to let the water out. Winding handles are generally fitted, or are hanging in readiness on hooks on the gates. As in England it is important to engage any safety ratchets before toiling at the *vannes* and to hang grimly onto the handle at all times, for its loss is not only dangerous but involves payment for a new one. I have seen a handle fly the length of

Descending the Meuse near Revin

a lock chamber when a ratchet slipped, fortunately without injury, for the man who had let go of it, the lock-keeper himself, was running like a rabbit at the time.

But this happens very, very rarely, and the commonest crisis is the discovery that the lock-keeper only oils the equipment on the side that he generally works himself. Two winding spindles are normally provided on each *vanne* but the one with lower gearing involves twice as many turns as the other, so the net result, of blood racing through the temples, is normally the same. After letting out the water and opening one of the gates, which is once again by winding, all that remains is for the crew to climb aboard down the ladder either in the chamber or in the gate itself, and to shout *merci beaucoup* as the boat departs.

Normally, when descending, we would drop a bight of rope over a bollard upon entering, merely as a reassurance that stopping short of the bottom gates was part of the plan. Then, having done so, we would often lift the noose back aboard again, for ropes have to be adjusted in descent, and are difficult to flick off once the boat has dropped. In any event the fall in a lock is usually gentle, and the boat may be controlled if needs be with the engine.

Ascending a lock is a different matter altogether, and on the return southwards from Revin the difference in tempo was most marked. Someone would have to scale the ladder each time we entered and receive a rope thrown by the steerer. It is surprising how adroit one becomes, although I once threw a noose over Bob Bennett's head and shoulders, so that he was compelled to gallop along the lockside wondering whether to brace himself as a bollard. Such incidents apart, we normally held the boat in place with the engine pulling in forward gear against this line, and were thus able to compete with the boiling inrush of water. Though by no means perfect, and with the obvious deficiency that the rope might break, I have found this method better than weaving a cat's cradle of lines. Putting the engine into gear also makes the tiller effective, and by keeping this hard over the boat remains pinned against one wall, rather than being slammed across

Leaving a lock. It speeds up the process if the gate winder from the crew is good at climbing down ladders. There is usually one located in the wall or in the back of the gate itself.

It is vital, I have found, to keep a variety of lines at hand, and to coil them through regularly, so that they may be used without snarling. It is also useful to be able to throw a rope, and although all of us from time to time will hurl a coil straight up, so that it falls back upon ourselves, a little practice helps. The secret is to coil the rope most carefully each time, no matter how urgent the situation, and if possible always coiling in the same direction, which is by convention clockwise. For maximum effect the thrower then holds a reasonable number of coils in one hand, takes half of them in the other, and throws those. With fortune the rope should then go out to its maximum extent.

At electric locks the keepers live a life of relative ease, but hand-winding men and women have a more strenuous existence and are prone to gripe at extra work. One of the things that drives them berserk, alas, is a succession of pleasure craft locking through separately, while the other lock-keeping obsession is time. The official hours of opening are adjusted according to the season, and in the summer they are long, from 6.30 in the morning until 7.30 at night, with a half-hour break for lunch. At the official hour in the evening the guillotine descends irrevocably,

into the other as the upstream *vannes* are lifted and the water races in.

With an electrically operated chamber everything depends on the keeper, and although those climbing ashore only have the rope to tend to, and no longer have to close a bottom gate as well, it is possible for the boat to be enclosed and the water let in before all is ready. This happened upon *Arthur's* return to Mézières, where the push-button man demonstrated the rapidity of his sluices with an uncalled-for grin. Fortunately we spotted a bollard recessed into the wall alongside, and a stout rope saved the day.

The lock-keeper works a thirteen hour day in summer, with a half-hour break for lunch and there is no concept of boatmen doing the work themselves, so that all traffic stops. Even more frustrating is the well-nigh universal tendency to say that 'this lock takes *x* minutes to operate; we cannot therefore permit any craft to enter at zero hour minus *x*.' The term *x* can be extended to as long as twenty minutes, and it is a powerful debater who can overcome this philosophy. Even the most persuasive fluent-French-speaking man who tips everybody will be thwarted by this universal adherence to the rules, and the net result is that you must then moor for the night, wherever the system dictates.

A much sillier variation concerns the authorized lunch break, which may be invoked when a boat is actually in the lock. As the official period is a mere half-hour, which is insufficient for lunch anywhere, let alone in France, it would seem wiser to spend an extra few moments winding handles in order to let a boat go. But then, some keepers argue, another vessel might turn up, and in general their flexibility on this matter depends on the amount of traffic. The whole thing is made more confusing by lunch being from 12 to 12.30 on certain canals, and from 12.30 to 1 pm on others.

These matters apart, *l'Entente Cordiale* is not too difficult to maintain.

Canal de l'Est, from Pont~ à~Bar to Troussey

176km (116 miles) and 40 locks

'*Eh, Henri, ici,*' hissed a small boy from a parapet. '*Voila Arthur . . . Arthur le Fantôme*'. It was on this waterway that I first heard that mysterious cry, and also met an old man with string around his knees and a Wyatt Earp moustache, which trembled with delight as he intoned the boat's name the way the French pronounce it, '*Artooor, Artooor*'. It

was his own name, and to judge from his excitement quite rare.

Later we discovered *Arthur le Fantôme* to be a strip cartoon hero in a minor way. It was pleasant to find that the name of the boat inspired such affection, and that we were not touring in the French equivalent of *Brutus* or *Oswald Moseley*. For this waterway runs through touchy country, the scene of many battles, while the Canal de l'Est itself was built after Germany annexed Alsace in 1871, and a new north-south link was needed in France to serve the industrial regions of Nancy and Toul.

The River Meuse is still incorporated south of Pont-à-Bar, and it can flood here too, despite the official insistence upon referring to the whole length from the border as the Canal de l'Est (branche Nord). Eventually as the voyager travels southward the lock cuts lengthen and the canal title becomes justified.

Sedan in the upper reaches is a military town and so, of course, is Verdun. Many battlefields are to be seen by the water, and earthworks and memorials and cemeteries. One of the lock houses is an old concrete bunker. Sedan itself, the site of the French capitulation in 1870, is an elegant town now, particularly by the river, although the grandeur of the fortress is somewhat dissipated by the car park at its foot and the prefabricated *Bureau de Tourism* which distributes news of guided tours. Further upstream is Stenay, where the German Crown Prince Wilhelm resided during the critical months of the Battle of Verdun in 1916. Here, a couple of days after *Arthur* had passed, the old weir across the river collapsed, effectively closing this route to traffic for a further five weeks.

At Verdun, where over half a million men died, monumental masonry and the upkeep of graveyards are major preoccupations. To cycle up to the main battlefield, inevitably in the pouring rain, is a sobering experience, for the plantations of pine woods do not conceal the mangled ground, while the exhibits of the fighting and further memorials at Douaumont fill whatever gaps the imagination has left. It is almost blasphemous in this context to mention that Verdun has quays at its very centre, and good moorings for yachts.

Weir north of Verdun. The Canal de l'Est incorporates many river sections.

Canal de l'Est, branche Sud, from Toul to Corre

147km (91 miles) and 99 locks

Lock under construction on the Moselle at Toul. With
completion of the river programme to Neuves Maisons,
the canals alongside are no longer used by through traffic,
the Moselle providing the main route.

For about twelve miles the Marne-Rhine route intervenes and then, for the voyager going south, the Canal
de l'Est is resumed. Once again there are splendid river
sections, this time taking in the upper reaches of the
Moselle. Apart from the odd trendy reach in which water
sports were practised, the river here was as unexploited
as the French Meuse — save that during *Arthur*'s visit the
river was being improved to take trains of barges propelled by pusher tugs. Further to the north and into
Germany the Moselle was already a rip-roaring commercial waterway where push-tow loads are an everyday
feature. Now, in its upstream reaches, we saw the first
signs of the new locks and the dredging programme
that have taken the traffic from the old Freycinet canals
alongside and put it onto the river instead.

The Canal de l'Est was built after the Franco-Prussian
war of 1870 and the surrender of lands further east,
including the route via the Rhine. It is thus of a recent
vintage by canal standards, and now it was being improved
once again. The goal for all this was the steelworks at
Neuves Maisons, a grim and 'H G Wellsian place, where
the orange smoke billows so thick it could be cut into
slices and used as mattress packing. By contrast the other
old ironworking villages of the area are quite attractive,
and most notably Sexey-aux-Forges, which stands on a
bend in the river. There a single winding street slopes
down towards the riverside, where a small cafe provides
the shmaltzy jukebox music that the French so love. Here
also is the traditional table football, at which it is fatal to
be challenged. Two local youths beat the *Arthur* team
10-nil, 9-1, 10-nil.

At Neuves Maisons itself we had the ill fortune to be
closeted in the lock for half an hour, having been foolish

Thereafter the route is less sombre, and passes through
unassuming countryside before reaching the cement works
of Sorcy and the junction with the Canal de la Marne au
Rhin just beyond.

Neuves Maisons

through the trees. The summit section itself, being both narrow and twisting, is a useful illustration of the necessity of proceeding with caution, for other craft lurk around such corners and hedgerows limit vision. It is primarily for this reason that flags are commonly flown from the bows of commercial vessels, and it behoves the careful pleasure boater to do the same, so that he can be seen a moment or two sooner. Whether these flags are national ensigns, burgees, or mere laundry is largely immaterial; they should merely be easy to see. The oil companies often give away bright little flags where fuel is bought, and these are commonly flown, while a dash of colour is often added to a bow coaming, as much for visibility as for decoration.

In fog, which is common in the early morning, it is customary for a *péniche* captain to put his granny or Uncle Dan up forward to peer earnestly into the gloom. Dim bow lights are also shown, so as not to dazzle, but these may be supplemented by a searing ray from the wheelhouse if needs be. During bad visibility it is particularly important to show a light when inside a lock, in order to forestall any delusion that the chamber might be empty and ready for some other vessel waiting just outside.

Halfway down towards the Saône we stumbled upon that most bemusing of all French canal phenomena, the emergency *chômage* or stoppage for repairs. These can strike like lightning, usually when things have been going rather well. Suddenly lock-keepers put their official hats on and, apart from a terse instruction that you can no longer proceed, they become remote and infuriatingly incommunicado. The only consolation is to find that the *péniches* which are piled up like an invasion fleet just ahead are no better informed either. Rumour spreads that the canal is blocked by a sunken barge, a crashed lorry, a landslide or a flood, and that it will take six hours, six days or six weeks to clear up the mess. Maintenance men roar up and down the towpath on autocycles, or in vans made of corrugated metal, but whatever their functions, the dissemination of information is not among them.

I have survived several emergency *chômages* in France, and although the nature of the calamity may differ, they all have one feature in common: that no-one bothers to

enough to enter two minutes before the dreaded lunch break. Nor would the seething lady keeper allow us to twirl a handle or raise a *vanne* until this period was over. Neuves Maisons is the only truly appalling spot on the whole canal, although there are stretches beyond which run a shade too close to the Route Nationale. But south of the short arm to Epinal the countryside closes in, and the Canal de l'Est quite literally takes to the backwoods.

Epinal, at the foot of the Vosges, is the centre of a region of hillocks and forests. Flights of locks take the canal to a summit level of 1200ft and spiral down again

Early morning mist. A good lookout is essential.

for rumour and for attempting to telephone England. The French family aboard the immaculate *Tajo*, lying loaded with china clay in the stretch below us, stolidly began to repaint their already gleaming craft. The Dutch and the Belgians, less philosophical, paced about the place and shouted. In the event we all stayed moored for five days.

When the new concrete was considered dry enough for traffic to proceed, we followed the *Tajo* past twenty-eight upcoming craft, with all the labour that passing involves. Hooters boomed through the woods; craft would sidle alongside one another and thrash the mud, before disengaging while one backed off to a hopefully wider spot for a further session. It takes time to travel like this. The canal through the Vosges is also stony, and in meeting loaded vessels which are reluctant to leave the centre channel pleasure craft must pass them very close, for the edges are shallow. In the interests of efficiency *Arthur* worked through each lock with a German sloop bound for the Costa Brava. The yacht drew four feet and had an echosounder, but despite this luxury struck bottom several times.

In contrast with the balmy Saône that follows, this last portion of the canal has a tight, enshrouded feeling as the water winds this way and that, occasionally passing dark

Diver at work during a *chômage*

provide enlightenment on cause or duration, and the only thing to do is to get off and walk, perhaps several miles if the hold-up is a big one, and look for yourself. On this particular occasion craft were being stopped one at each lock and made to stay there — a wise decision in view of the mayhem customary after a *chômage*, when everybody tries to set off at once. As a result however, craft were draped in line across many miles of remote countryside, in some cases so far from shops and supplies that a flying doctor service could scarcely have coped.

A wall had collapsed ten locks further down, weakening a gate in the process. A little nearer stood a cafe, a base

Emergency closure: the lock-keeper returns to other duties

question to tie to trees, or to the towpath; that you cannot turn your boat around and go back the way you have come during a *chômage*, since *all* movement is prohibited; that a boat may not lie on the same side as a cafe, since that is by the towpath, but must endure the concentrated patch of nettles opposite. Nor may a vessel be attached to a concrete signpost, however stout (*Arthur* had his name taken for doing this). Furthermore, although we were generously allowed to pass through a lock on the threshold of lunch hour, we were compelled to moor just beyond, lest the next keeper, who was also an overseer, might deduce that the earlier infraction had taken place. The speed limit of six kilometres an hour along the summit section is rigidly enforced by checking times on the telephone. In view of all this, it is to the credit of those lady and gentlemen officers on the *branche Sud* who remain cheery in the face of so much barrack-room lawyerism all around.

mansions with high railings, sometimes affording glimpses of the accompanying river, the Coney. My own memories are of dark green forests steaming in the rain, with lock following lock, each hand-wound, and with a pile of sawn logs beside each one, as if anticipating total isolation from the world outside.

It may be my own peculiar fortune, but the Southern Branch is also etched on my brain as a place of rules, regulations and edicts, all enforced in the same Jobsworth vein of the English caretaker ('Honestly guv, it's more than me job's worth . . .'). With great fervour I have been variously informed that it is forbidden to moor near a lock, even for the two minutes desired; that it is out of the

The Saône from Corre to St-Symphorien

158km (98 miles) and 20 locks

The glorious upper reaches of this river can be compared to the Thames during the nineteenth century. If symbols are needed they can be found in the lazy-faced cattle, wallowing in the heat of the day, in the placid angler immobile in his skiff, or in the tall trees on the bank through which the wind hisses and sighs. The most up-to-date intrusion during *Arthur*'s visit was provided by a vintage steam locomotive with high smokestack and a shrieking whistle, which suddenly shot into view alongside the water at the head of a line of trucks. We exchanged frantic waves with the enginemen before tucking into one of the several lock cuts.

The Canal de l'Est on the descent towards the Saône

The Saône in summer. There are trees almost all the way.

These short canal sections illustrate the wisdom of obeying the notice boards provided by the navigation authorities. If a sign appears on the bank indicating a speed limit of six kilometres an hour, then it is ten to one that around the corner there will be a sharp turn-off at the head of a weir, or perhaps just a lock, with the piers of a railway bridge to forestall any further manoeuvres. There are two alternatives in such a case: to go hard astern and to trust that the boat does not swing broadside in the process; or to descend the weir in a shower of wooden sticks and the flimsy metal girders that support them. So it is at Conflandey, the fourth lock down from the Canal

de l'Est, and it is amazing that such incidents do not regularly occur.

Otherwise the Saône is wide and mellow, a beautiful river, with the occasional slumbering village across the water meadows, or the rare small town. In keeping with the atmosphere, the keepers are friendly, kindly men, regardless of whether or not their lock has been selected for electrification. The Saône is an ancient navigation, which like so many in France, was modernized in the second half of the nineteenth century. This is evidenced in the grey stonework and the directness of some of the cuts, which shorten the journey by forging across the neck of some great loop in the river, sometimes by means of tunnels, with porticos arranged like some triumphal dais at a stadium.

The tunnels are at St-Albin (681m) and Savoyeux (643m) and they are guarded by traffic lights which remain at red a considerable time, for account must also be taken of traffic at locks beyond. Thus the voyager is controlled by an administrator who is well out of view, and who relies on an obscure system of microphones mounted on poles in order to tell him the state of play. Whether or not captains are expected to shout into them in passing is unclear; certainly I never have.

For those voyaging downstream, the tunnels are preceded by another long cut or *dérivation* through Port-sur-Saône, a small town where the main road crosses at an extremely awkward bend. The crew of *Arthur* observed this awkwardness by watching, with fingers to ears, as a Belgian *péniche* with engine howling hard astern thundered into one of the abutments in the dusk. The stonework shook as if it were rubber and many windows were flung open in the houses alongside. It is widely held along the waterways that it is the Belgians who always hit things, as they are the great floggers-on into the night, presumably in a steady rage, for lock hours in France are shorter and more rigid than in Belgium.

While the primary cause in this case was undoubtedly that the *péniche* was travelling too fast, it was supplemented by a strong current – caused by drawing off at the lock down below – and by a reef of mud, which makes steering any vessel difficult. Torches were being deployed in the darkness to see if the vessel had sprung a leak, but amazingly no mark could be seen on the bow. Quite what causes the enormous dents that are occasionally seen is outside comprehension.

As the valley widens, further elegant towns appear; Gray, Pontailler and Auxonne, at each of which is a quay comprising a continuous flight of long steps or terraces which continue down to, and beneath, the surface of the Saône. Mooring at these demands some caution, in order to avoid grounding on one of the shelves, and the normal procedure is to prop the boat out somehow with long spars and a web of lines. Many lizards and the occasional rat live on these steps, and although all these scatter as the first ropes are dramatically hurled ashore, they re-appear as soon as silence descends. But never, in my experience, has a rat come aboard. And so it is possible to leave the boat, and go off to shop or eat.

Shopping and Eating

Eating is one of the theoretical attractions of France, and like shopping it is subject to a number of variables. Most boats settle into a regular style of life aboard, dictated by what is easily available and what is not, and a run through the pattern on *Arthur* may give a few helpful guidelines.

Breakfast aboard the *Arthur* can be a morose affair, depending on the degree of celebration the day before. With a supreme effort of will this can be counteracted by rising very early, starting the engine and entering the next lock with a few biffs and bangs to sharpen the wits of anyone remaining down below.

Our lunches, taken later, will generally be of salad, accompanied by a discussion on the merits of various cheeses, *paté* and wine. Wine is sold in various grades in France, rather in the manner of petrol. *Douze* is the best of the *vins ordinaires*, though slightly more expensive

Weir at Conflandey, with lock in the background

Tunnel at Savoyeux, cutting across a great loop in the river. The traffic is controlled by lights.

than passable *onze*. *Dix* is pretty rough, though *neuf-et-demi* can be found sometimes, which is dreadful. All are much sharper than the cheap wines bought in England, and they lack that strange heavy taste as of boiled-up cinema cushions that is to be found in the wines at London parties.

Likewise butter, chicken, and eggs all taste different and better in France, presumably because they have not been deep-frozen, kept in cages, or derived from fowl on insipid diets. As other members of the European Community revile the inefficient French farmers let us remember that French food still tastes of something.

Patés are less well documented. The mark of a good one is that it gets ravenned to extinction in half a meal, and must then be supplemented by germ warfare masquerading as cheese. *Paté* varies enormously in price, and not all the expensive ones are satisfying, particularly to palates coarsened by *vin ordinaire*. The *patés de campagne* found in all *charcuteries* are quite adequate and sufficiently varied for most tastes.

I dwell on all this in answer to the questions most commonly asked. The canal life does not force people to feed on berries, leaves or TV dinners. French foodstuffs are excellent in an unwrapped, non-desiccated, unsteamed and generally unmolested way. In villages there are good general stores while the larger towns sport supermarkets of a most superior quality, often with counters entirely devoted to cheese, or meat, or fruit, which in the universal way of self-service stores is served by assistants. But there are pitfalls. Shops are open on Sundays, naturally, lest people might starve; but as a result, and quite disastrously for the unwary, French shopkeepers and restauranteurs take Mondays off in order to recover. Nor is it possible to shop between 12 and 2pm or perhaps 2.30, as the shopkeepers themselves have to eat.

When travelling by boat it is difficult to be in the right place at the right time to take account of these arrangements. The lock-keepers often sell eggs or vegetables, but usually confine themselves to one or two basic commodities, such as leeks, which are put on display by the canalside and for which it is customary to barter in a

Lunchtime aboard *Arthur*, looking forward towards the entrance to the old boatman's cabin in the bow

civilized sort of way. Alternatively, in the remoter regions there are travelling shops, but as their times are erratic and as there is a general horror of labelling their outsides, stopping one of these can be fraught and difficult.

For similar sorts of reasons, eating out is not always easy. The restaurant ten kilometres down the canal or river might have been a restaurant the last time a lock-keeper visited it, but that may have been during the war, possibly even the First War, and the chances are that it is a tobacconist's now. In any event, with other traffic ahead, it is conceivable that further locks might close before this promised Nirvana can be reached. Thus eating out demands some planning. We used the *Guide Michelin* a little, but this tended to shoot rather high, into the realms of pretension rather than jollity, and our best successes on *Arthur* stemmed from mooring early and scouring the town on bicycles – sometimes sending further parties on foot to search the town for the scourers.

It generally proves wisest to stop at the first recognizable berth, since the proverbial better one rarely appears if you go on to look for it. It is unthinkable in France to

At the lockside. On the rural canals many lock-keepers also
run smallholdings.

retrace your steps through locks and swing-bridges should
the place you had passed earlier be considered a more
desirable mooring after all.

The best food is found between 7 and 7.30, the
customary times of serving, save in the south, when
meals are sometimes later; and the real successes often
come with ordering the most expensive meal on the menu
of a relatively cheap restaurant. The converse approach
is invariably disastrous. At 1972 prices, the crew of
Arthur got excellent fare at 16 francs, haughty service and
miserable portions at 38. For non-linguists some kind of
basic dictionary is useful, and they need not then be sur-
prised if *cailles* prove to be tiny little birds just recently
descended from their nests.

Bars, of course, are as much a French institution as
restaurants, and those beside the water often have the
advantage of being well clear of the Routes Nationales.
There is such a place at St-Symphorien, where the Rhone-
Rhine Canal joins the Saône. Here the countryside is flatter
and the valley broadened, so that it is possible to sit before
the tiny clutch of buildings at this point, sipping wine
and gazing across a vast countryside as if one owned it all.

Canal du Rhône au Rhin

237km (147 miles) and 119 locks

An old waterway with relatively little traffic, this route is
often colloquially referred to as 'The Doubs', for many of
the western stretches incorporate that majestic, craggy
river. Upon first entry at St-Symphorien there are canal
sections which are pleasant enough, save for a quaint
prohibition against mooring from a point a kilometre up,
until two automatic locks have been passed. Full details
are provided by the keeper at St-Symphorien, a cheery
soul with a Winston Churchill-jolly-good-chap line of
repartee. Since the first two *biefs*, or stretches between
locks, are so attractive, and as the prohibited section that
follows concludes at an ugly factory, it is wiser to stay at
St-Symphorien for the night.

The automatic locks are automatic no longer, and
although provision was once made for gates to shut and
water to enter at the mere pull of a string, for some reason
this system has not been a success. Little electric lecterns
have now been provided instead, so that the keepers can
jab at push-buttons with their thumbs. As *Arthur* has been
present when a thumb hit the wrong button, I feel quali-
fied to warn that craft should be firmly attached to the
shoreside bollards.

Almost all the other locks are hand-winders, of a crude
and primitive kind. *Vannes* are activated by long levers,

The River Doubs

the sluices themselves being large butterfly valves not unlike the choke of a carburetter. Anyone sitting on the bow of an ascending boat thus has a split second vision of a mighty jet of water two feet in diameter and hurtling towards him as the lever is swung at the lockside up above.

Once the marshlands have been cleared, the town of Dôle is reached, a lovely old place, and nowhere more so than from the river, for here the Doubs is joined. There are good moorings overlooked by the handsome church and tight-packed town. Just across the small tannery canal Louis Pasteur was born, and there is a remarkable conjunction of walkway and water around the old mill —

converted into an expensive discotheque upon my last arrival, but still attractive outside.

Upstream of Dôle is a section of canal so enshrouded by trees that the water is a constant shade of green. It is followed shortly by Rochefort-sur-Nenon, where cliffs tower above the water. Here the narrow canal section debouches suddenly into the river once again, inevitably just above a weir. Such cuts are well known among the boat people, who take a rather melodramatic view of the Doubs, and they are the cause of much hooting by craft wafting downstream.

Further hazards take the form of large tables of rock which lie in the river bed. There are frequent maps at the lockside to show these, although it is at first difficult to discover whether they relate to reaches above or below each lock (in fact they show the stretches below). If in doubt, and there is a fair amount of doubt on the Doubs, it pays to first talk things over with each keeper. But, save after heavy rain, the Doubs need not be terrifying to those in shallow draft craft. A useful rule of thumb is to steer close to the towpath. Close means really close, say fifteen to twenty yards, which may seem almost like steering up the bank when contrasted with the width of the river; but the distance makes better sense when the old function of the towpath is recalled, for however long the towlines, boats would naturally bear close in when heading upstream in a current.

The Doubs scenery merits many superlatives. Chiefly it comprises rocky but densely wooded hillsides through which the river winds tightly. There are many stretches to recommend: the narrows near Osselle, the short tunnel at Thoraise, and all the reaches that follow, right up to the fortress at Besançon.

Besançon is an exuberant university town located in a big sweep of the river. The old citadel, built by Vauban under Louis XIV, stands on the high isthmus and under this a tunnel has more recently been cut for water traffic. Two locks provide access, the second one actually within the tunnel, but the best mooring is in between, down the arm that once conducted barges around the town. Moorings at the upstream end of the tunnel are poor, there

The church of Notre-Dame at Dôle. Pasteur's birthplace is among the houses in the foreground.

A canal section just above Dôle. Further eastwards and upstream the river is entered.

The tunnel at Thoraise. Craft emerging here must turn abruptly. The tunnel itself cuts under a peninsula.

being only the faded wharves of the old port at which to lie. The locks following are alongside basic, uncontrollable weirs, into which it is possible for gate winders to plummet, as the locksides are narrow, with sundry obstacles. The keepers vary; sometimes old men, occasionally pretty girls, and at one point the original Charles Addams family.

When the main road is not alongside, the river is as magnificent above Besançon as it is below, but gradually it yields itself to canal, and thus by way of the manufacturing town of Montbeliard and the junction with an arm to Belfort, the watershed is reached.

Beyond the summit the waterway changes completely, as Alsace is entered. Slices of sausage are offered and the German influence is most marked. There are many locks, the first twenty-one in a more or less continuous flight. One keeper had electrified the *vannes* with an ingenious system of belts and pulleys; another worked his with the aid of a heavy-duty drill and a long piece of electrical wire. The rest are hand-winders.

There are plans to link the Rhine and the Saône with a new wide canal, passing over the same hilly territory but capable of taking much larger craft and reducing the journey time from five days to thirty-six hours. The scale of these intended works can be seen beyond Mulhouse, pronounced 'Mullooze', a stylish town with the canal in a striking avenue. From just beyond the housing a new cut of awe-inspiring dimensions has already been built towards the Rhine. This is the Embranchement de Kembs-Niffer, which in eight miles features just one bend. So wide is this canal that it is easy to misjudge the distance. The banks are concreted and sloping; the scenery, such as is visible, is mere scrubland.

A lock stands at the end giving access into the Grand Canal d'Alsace, which is really the canalized Rhine. The *péniches*, which have laboured over from the Saône, wait nearby to clear Customs, for the lock is also a border point with Germany across the river and Switzerland just upstream. There is paperwork here, but not much: merely a look at passports, a joke or two about the photos therein, and stamping the Green Card. But the waterway beyond carries heavy traffic both night and day, with uncertain moorings, so that anyone wishing to stop for a while is recommended to stay in the Rhône au Rhin.

The Doubs locks stand directly alongside the weirs and descending in times of flood demands caution and a powerful hooter to warn the keepers to prepare. This is the last river section before Besançon. The citadel stands on the skyline.

On the Grand Canal d'Alsace near Breisach

Kembs to Strasbourg

125km (78 miles) and 20 locks

At enormous expense the Rhine's upper reaches have been canalized, so that Basel is now a major port. This has been achieved by blasting a wide artificial waterway, Le Grand Canal d'Alsace, down the stark and empty plain, occasionally letting the original river join in for a few metres or so. Scenery is scarce, apart from a brief view of the Black Forest at Breisach, virtually the only

place with a sheltered mooring. There are wild duck in many reaches as nowhere else in France, presumably because the canal is too wide for accurate gunnery from its shores.

'Hello sailors' cried a Dutchman from a 2000-tonner as it stomped out of a lock beside our own, and as three more craft followed him, we felt very small fry indeed. The locks are enormous and up to fifty feet deep, which strikes you very forcibly when you've got to return down a ladder after stopping off to take photographs.

On such mighty waterways it is the custom to hover a good distance from the locks while waiting to see which of the two chambers is being prepared to receive traffic – and also to keep well clear of assorted cargo vessels as they manoeuvre into position one after another. A pair of binoculars is most handy for interpreting light signals which, although featuring many bulbs, are obscure in the daytime. As in so many places, red lights mean 'do not enter', green 'enter now', and a mixture of both 'I know you are there and will shortly be doing something about it'.

The keepers conduct conversations in German through a line of loudspeakers down the bank, and craft reply through amplification, all of which is most disconcerting in fog. Traffic continues at all times day and night, but boats without radar must cower at a mooring when visibility is poor. Unhappily, tying-up facilities are not generally provided, save alongside a battered scow above each lock, obviously put there as an afterthought. Once again the banks take the form of concrete slopes where waves splash up and down continuously. The wash of the passing leviathans conjures up visions of the Dogger Bank in a storm, and there is little recourse but to lie alongside the old boat provided. There a notice ominously proclaims that these moorings are not for craft longer than 38.50m. While lying at Ottmarsheim, *Arthur* had two laden *petroliers* alongside, tanker *péniches* bristling with notices about smoking. Though brought beautifully to their mooring, they provided fairly robust company in the occasional surges during the night.

Pleasure craft are largely ignored, which saves messy tipping sessions at the locks. The chief obligation is to

In the lock at Rhinau. Another vessel is alongside the *Wartenberg*; several more are astern.

moor in the chamber as quickly as possible, so that traffic is not delayed. A klaxon sounds when the sluices are about to be drawn, causing some surprise to those standing immediately in front of the loudspeaker. Thereafter, it is merely a question of staying attached to the bollards, which are generally of the floating type, sliding down on rails as the water level drops and avoiding the necessity for adjustment. The lower lock gates lift guillotine fashion, decanting streams of water upon those departing beneath, so that even on a fine day rainwear can be useful.

Although an international waterway, and free of charge to all users, this part of the Rhine navigation is adminis-tered from France. Alongside the locks are hydroelectric dams, and this vast work, which involves eight locks, was completed only in 1971. Previously the main river was turbulent and fast-running. At that time the old Canal du Rhône au Rhin continued alongside all the way to Strasbourg, and although much of this has now been taken out of use, the crew of the *Arthur* happily discovered that one part remained. Having descended the Rhine in a combination of wind and sun that dulled the senses, we had foolishly entered the lock at Rhinau first. This brought the keeper down to ask how wide *Arthur* was (it is useful to know – to the nearest centimetre) in order to squeeze two enormous vessels alongside. In the process he was able to tell us that the old Freycinet canal to Stras-bourg still remained open with an entry from just below that particular lock.

After the furies of the Grand it was like going into the Wurzel Gummidgeshire Tub Boat Canal. Suddenly a *péniche* waterway seemed very small and comforting, and if this old line cut rather straight and had many more locks, it also had banks that could be tied to, and even the occasional café. A nodding Customs officer sat as custodian to this byway, re-sorting the papers of the five or so commercial craft that passed each day and stamping the Green Cards of the more infrequent 'yacht'. Maize grows in the fields nearby, but is not to be trusted. Apart from the risk of apprehension, there is little to be savoured in the French variety which remains rock-hard like a cluster of marbles, and resists all cooking. It is customarily fed to cattle.

The city of Strasbourg, famed as a political and com-mercial fulcrum, is encircled by waterways. Those making the speedier journey via the Grand Canal d'Alsace pass through the extensive docks. Craft arriving by the back door, like ourselves, take a circuit of canals about half a mile from the city centre. For the knowledgeable, a passage of the narrow and fast-running River Ill leads to a whim-sical mooring at the very heart, with half-timbered build-ings worthy of any jigsaw puzzle. There are connections between the Ill and the commercial waters around, but at the time of my own arrival I did not know them. We

Rhine traffic is continuous, operating both day and night

Canal de la Marne au Rhin

Strasbourg to Vitry, 313km (194 miles) and 171 locks

A hill and dale affair, this waterway first passes through the cuckoo-clock villages of Alsace and ends at the canal town of Vitry-le-François, where the cooking is very much better. The plain near Strasbourg is fairly dull, save on a Sunday, when waterborne jousting is practised. This popular sport involves teams of rowers who make towards one another to the accompaniment of music from the shore. When the music stops, the oars are lifted and two jousters on platforms lunge at each other with padded poles. As soon as one falls in, another rower moves up to take his place. A commentator keeps the tally and enthuses the crowd, halting the show for a moment or two whenever some other vessel appears through the bridge. The most elaborate form of this tournament is held down at Sète, on the Mediterranean coast, but the sport is practised in Germany and Italy as well as France. As seen outside Strasbourg it looks tough and debilitating.

At Saverne the canal passes before a large chateau. A maintenance wharf opposite affords a useful mooring, and also several piles of sand in which to play *boules*. Proper *boules*, the simple but skilful game played all over France, involves hard balls tossed underhand towards a jack. The nearest throw wins, but the knocking away of rival balls is part and parcel of the game. *Boules* can be played almost anywhere, but with inferior balls such as tourists tend to buy the bright plastic of which they are made leads them to bounce. It is then most useful to have piles of sand or gravel on which to throw and these are conveniently provided at the wharves of the Department of Bridges and Highways, which maintains the canals.

There are many locks on the canal, all electrified, and

were committed instead to a seedy stopping point beside the inner ring road. Here the only item of any consequence at all is one of the old electric mules, on exhibition in a glass case near l'Ecluse de l'Hôpital, at a point of maximum invisibility. For those brave enough to cross the highway, the centre of this revered city is one kilometre distant.

Sunday morning sport on the Canal de la Marne au Rhin.
Waterborne jousting is widely popular.

caisson raises and lowers vessels sideways on a ramp. For pleasure craft, the service is entirely free and the motion is so smooth it is anticlimatic, the man on duty there selling postcards during *Arthur*'s five minutes in the tank.

In the winding house is a reproduction from a technical magazine, describing not only the Arzviller plane but the one at Foxton in Leicestershire which preceded it in 1900, carrying two narrow boats at a time up to the Grand Union summit until abandonment in 1911 and the final dismantling in 1927. Foxton has gone now, but Arzviller is of the space age, looking very slick and Dan Dare-ish. It was built as a small scale model of further lifts projected for the new route between Rhine and Saône, but the decision has since been taken to use conventional locks instead, the complication and uncertainties of expense probably being the deciding factors. One of the biggest problems at Arzviller itself was the cutting of a new section of canal at the upper end. This slices through orange rock on the lip of the hillside, from which the traveller can look down on the old locks that it once took over half a day to climb.

Maintenance wharves provide a good space
for playing *boules*

although it was said that the canal was 'dying' there was ample enough traffic during my own visit, with an average of one *péniche* for every lock.

West of Saverne the landscape becomes more wooded and tighter, culminating in a final ascent at Arzviller. Here stands the principal feature of the Marne au Rhin, an inclined plane for transporting boats to and from the summit level. Built at a cost of 60 million francs, it was opened in 1969, replacing seventeen locks which stand derelict nearby. It is a major tourist attraction, with sightseers ignoring the various notices of interdiction to teeter on the very edge of the concrete abyss. A single

Saverne. The boat is a converted Dutch sailing cargo vessel.

There are several tunnels on the Marne au Rhin, two being quite near the lift. These are 2307m and 475m long, officially with towing by electric loco, although if no other craft are present a 'yacht' may be permitted to go through under her own steam. If doing this, it is necessary to pause between the two tunnels in order to pass the tow or *râme* travelling in the opposite direction. Attractions here are expresses on the main line railway near at hand, many wild flowers in the cuttings, and grasshoppers the size of miniature cigars. At the eastern end of Arzviller tunnel stands a memorial stone to a young man drowned in 1854.

For many miles beyond the canal passes through villages where old wharves still remain, as shown in the strip maps of the *Guide*. Invariably these little rural basins are shallow, and a certain amount of bulldozing of silt is called for in order to reach the bank at all. Excavation on the wharf itself sometimes reveals an old bollard or ring; otherwise tying up is a major problem, with the only recourse the leading of long lines to some distant telegraph pole or tree. The countryside is pleasant, but apart from some fine lakes concealed by embankments near the junction with the branch to the Sarre, the views are by French standards unremarkable. Kites and buzzards fly overhead in certain spots, while flowers, butterflies and wild plants may be seen as everywhere. After travelling around the system a few weeks, it comes as a shock to realize how such sights have become a commonplace.

Nancy has a reputation as an industrial centre, but apart from a brief flourish of activity at Dombasle and a mile or two of suburb, the squalor is not excessive. In fact Nancy sports some of the finest baroque architecture in France. The Place Stanislas, now happily cleared of parked cars, provides a sensation of town life as it ought to be. A series of palaces surround the square, and at a slight angle down a street beyond is the twin-towered cathedral. Heavily ornamented and guilded fountains play in the corners, while there are several cafés on the Parisian pattern, although the city lacks the hardness of Paris itself.

The canal runs close at hand, through a series of basins lined with craft, for several other routes join nearby. To the west is a short spur into the Moselle, another international waterway. As part of its further modernization and extension up towards Toul and the steelworks of Neuves Maisons, the plan has been to put all traffic into the river and to abandon the Marne au Rhin alongside. During *Arthur*'s visit this work was still incomplete, and we were able to cross the Moselle by an aqueduct due to be demolished when the river takes over. Just across stands Liverdun, a quaint village with a further short tunnel bored beneath. With modernisation, traffic now follows the river, and craft call at Liverdun no more.

Fairs are a feature of France. We had already experienced

The Arzviller inclined plane, bypassing seventeen locks.
A *péniche* is descending in the caisson.

Counterbalance weights pass beneath the caisson, and many
safety devices are incorporated. Operation takes a matter
of minutes.

The Place Stanislas at Nancy. The statue is of Stanislaus Leszczynski, the dethroned King of Poland who ruled Lorraine in the eighteenth century and rebuilt much of the town.

one at Hochfelden, one of the prim Germanic towns near Strasbourg. But that at Toul overshadowed it. Every so often the entire old walled town is given over to a market and fun fair of the most rumbustious kind. French dodgem cars are the fastest in the world, the liquorice the most varied. But there are many other delights: salesmen of the Lancashire market type, donkey rides, beat groups, ladies telling fortunes, gentlemen selling everything from wine barrels to motorbikes. People come from miles around in fleets of buses exotically entitled *Les Rapides de la Meuse* or whatever. Frequently there are band displays, stunning in their incompetence but conducted with

Tows pass at Mauvages (*Albert Barber*)

Entering the tunnel (*Albert Barber*)

splendid gravity in elaborate uniforms. As buglers blow their ragged volleys the thumping of the bass drum resounds around the walls. The themes tend towards martial incentive and glory, but there is sporadic dancing, before the last bus leaves and the final leather-jacketed revellers clamber upon their Hondas and whine away into the night.

There were similar festivities farther on, at Bar-le-Duc, the home of the bicycle, but here as an added attraction the heavily publicized Jean Sunny and his team drove motocars on two wheels, and through fire. These and other manoeuvres were all performed in front of a boggling crowd restrained from the theatre of events by a cursorily erected length of string.

Between Toul and Bar-le-Duc lie many more locks and two further tunnels. One, the Souterrain de Foug, *Arthur* had already passed through in the reverse direction while journeying between the two separated halves of the Canal de l'Est. Foug is a short tunnel, with towing whenever traffic materializes by means of electric mule. The other tunnel, at Mauvages on the summit level, is 4877m long, that is just over 3 miles, and accordingly it is taken most seriously. Sheets printed in several languages itemize the various requirements for towing through by chain tugs: that 'yachts' go to the rear of the *râme*; that they be adequately fendered and provide their own towing cable to the vessel ahead; that the signal in emergency be long and powerful blasts on the hooter, but that otherwise everyone must be reasonably silent; that motors should not be run within the tunnel; that anyone who touches the overhead wires does so at his peril; and so on.

There was only one other westbound vessel waiting, the loaded *Imelda* from Nancy, but the eastbound *râme* promised the maximum quota of ten or eleven vessels, that being the number capable of working through the locks on the other side between departures of the tug.

An emerging *râme* is a most dramatic spectacle. First of all a distant rumbling can be heard from within the tunnel, and this continues for half an hour or so before the clanking of the chain may be heard and the box-like tug looms into view. As each *péniche* appears, husband, wife and family start mopping off debris fallen from the tunnel

Drifting along in the tow. Lights illuminate the path alongside.

roof, shouting to one another, wielding hoses and brushes, and walking down the deck to keep station with those waiting to enter in the other direction. Engines thunder into life, before dropping back to a tickover. At Mauvages, the eastern portal is just before a bend which the tug cannot negotiate, and so for a further two hundred yards electric mules are brought into use until the tail of the *râme* has cleared the tunnel. The water swirls, towing cables drop with a hiss, to be coiled down with leather-gloved hands. Then the last messages are passed as the leading boats head away.

By contrast the passage within the tunnel is tranquil, drifting along on the towrope, with the occasional light passing overhead. Lunch is prepared on the vessel in front; the tug clanks distantly beyond; there is a general atmosphere of trance. Mauvages is now the second longest tunnel in use on the French canals, being 800m shorter than Bony, and so bright is the light upon emerging that it takes several seconds to acknowledge that the day is overcast, or even raining. Once again there is clamour. On the line of craft waiting to enter there are shouts to the tugmen that the next *râme* must depart *tout de suite*. The calls were particularly vociferous upon our own emergence at Mauvages for some time earlier the canal bank had collapsed down near Vitry, and many of the *péniches* had suffered long delays awaiting a repair. As the *Imelda* muscled past in the opposite direction, the captain, a taciturn soul, raised an arm in greeting as he slid past one group after another, while his wife shouted gossip from the stern. Two hundred craft had been delayed by the accident and all of these we would have to pass on the descent. Of the craft waiting for the tunnel, some had been delayed at the breach for eight days.

1972, the year in which I passed through Mauvages, was also the time in which the canals of central France showed real signs of wear and tear. Like some faithful jersey that suddenly gives at the sleeves, holes began to appear and the fabric no longer looked so trusty. Besides the weir that collapsed on the Meuse, another had gone at Marolles on la Petite Seine, while the burst bank near Vitry, with its enormous accumulation of craft, had

Boat operation is a family affair, with children joining in during the holidays.

The boatman works a long day. On the smaller canals some
eighty per cent are owner-operators, independent of large
concerns.

attracted scandalized comment in the *Journal de la Naviga-*
tion, the boat people's newspaper. The theme was that not
enough money was being spent, and that a backlog of maintenance, or rather of non-maintenance, had finally overtaken the smaller waterways.

This is not to say that these breaches were not repaired;
in fact the patching up was executed with great dexterity
by the staff on hand, in the remarkable space of nine days.
It was merely that the 350-ton *péniche* canals standardized
under the Freycinet Act of 1879 were seen to be in decline.

The families who operate the *péniches* have for some
time been despondent at an apparent lack of interest in
their welfare. While showpieces like the Rhine or the new
locks on the River Oise were getting good publicity, these
were for the 1350-ton 'Europe'-sized barges, generally
operated by large companies, or for great pusher trains
operated on an impersonal, computerized basis. Some
eighty per cent of the *péniches* are owned by the families
who work them and these recent trends and the apparent
uninterest of governments committed to the more flam-
boyant forms of technology were posing a threat to
thousands of people and the agreeable lifestyle they re-
present. The signs of pressure have been there for some
time: of boat people working for every available minute,
once they have obtained a load; of the central canals
becoming proportionately more neglected as the traffic
declines on them; of craft travelling part-laden; and of
long queues at the freight *bureaux*. The process need not
be inevitable, and there are several fairly obvious reasons
as to why this traffic should continue. It can be argued that
all water transport is civilized, and *efficient enough*.

After any such hold-up there are often further delays
along a canal, for craft must pass one another and await
their turn at the locks. And so it was on the Marne au
Rhin, all the way down through Ligny and Bar-le-Duc,
past the spot where an old steam piledriver was still
making good the damage, and to Vitry-le-François itself,
another small town in the interior, where the line of the
River Marne is joined.

Working hard to leave the lock – an exact fit on the Freycinet canals

Vitry to Berry~au~Bac

106km (66 miles) and 35 locks

Another chain of waterways leads from Vitry-le-François towards the Aisne. The first of these for the traveller heading northwards is the Latéral à la Marne, which for the most part is hypnotically straight. There are many small and venomous insects in this region and they sell their lives dearly. Châlons-sur-Marne, however, is a civilized place, a centre for champagne with a cathedral dating from the seventeenth century and with shady walks beneath the trees by the waterside. With a modern shopping centre, typical of France, Châlons also offers everything material, although I would caution against French clothes. It is small wonder that French people mount coach and air-charter parties purely to shop at Marks & Spencers, for their own apparel is often ill-fitting and tends to shrink. Buttondown fronts take up a scallop formation after the very first wash; collars project like the wreckage of a Sopwith Camel, and it is not unusual for the two halves of a shirt front to be of different lengths.

The River Marne itself runs near to the canal at Châlons, a small stream at this point although later to become a navigation of great charm, and the quickest way into Paris. Unhappily it was *chômagé* during *Arthur*'s visit, an act of apparent madness in view of the build-up of traffic after the burst near Vitry, but the officially laid down timetable for repairs is not easily departed from in France. As a result there were many delays, with fuming Belgians prominent among the assorted *batelliers* still caught in the hold-up.

As an illustration of the delays that persist after a canal closure, *Arthur* journeyed five km and through four locks between midday and canal closure time at 7.30. This was entirely caused by the press of traffic ahead, and the long time it takes whenever loaded boats meet craft heading in the opposite direction. Nor can the voyager just tie to the bank and fall asleep, for others in a similar plight will then overtake. In such situations it is not uncommon for three or four vessels to be hovering in line astern waiting for the next lock, and extremely tedious all this is.

Happily, the southern end of the Canal de l'Aisne à la Marne, in which so many were compelled to wait so long, is one of the few exhilarating sections along the route. There are clear views across a great rolling countryside, with blue-grey hills in the background and a zip in the air that makes the heart pound. After the marshes of the upper Marne valley it is inspiring to be able to see for miles, without poles or pylons or lights.

A further tunnel, that of Billy-le-Grand, offers locomo-

Leaving the tunnel at Billy-le-Grand, near Reims (*Robert Shopland*)

ring roads. With great determination it is possible to reach that edge remotest from the action and to stay for the night. Well outside the town stands the new port, a busy commercial centre but not a good spot to moor.

A short succession of further locks must perforce be taken slowly in times of great congestion. They lead to Berry-au-Bac, the point on the route to the Ardennes covered in an earlier chapter.

The Aisne and the Oise

Berry-au-Bac to Conflans-Ste-Honorine, 190km (118 miles) and 20 locks

The River Aisne flows through gravel pit country, so it comes as no surprise at a wharf to find yourself surrounded by a group of toughies who ought to be advertising bitter ale. These are gravel loaders, such as may be encountered on the Canal Latéral à l'Aisne, which flows westwards to meet the river at the two staircase locks at Celles. Although worthy of some movie about the Australian outback, as they lean on their shovels and spit, the gravel loaders are fairly amenable fellows, more given to courteous enquiry than their demeanour might suggest. The foreman of a group met on the canal section was embarrassingly torn between putting his men to work and demonstrating his knowledge of English, which was considerable. English speaking Frenchmen are something of a rarity and it transpired that our friend had spent several years working on an American base, which explained his accent and an unfortunate choice of adjectives. He advised us to stop at Soissons, 'a . . . . great town', out on the river itself.

Soissons is hardly great, although there is a good quay on the broad river and a Rubens in the cathedral. For the rest of its course the Aisne is a friendly waterway, with overhanging trees and attractive villages. At the township of Attichy I saw a compatible aggregation of small infants,

tive haulage for a distance of 2302m, and a charge (9.22 francs when *Arthur* passed through) whether pleasure craft are towed or not. As there was much other traffic we took the tow, behind the Belgian *Daniel*, the *S-D* bound for Le Havre, and the *Actif*, which played wild pop music throughout. Those aboard busied themselves polishing that which was already polished, and fiddling with a flag-staff grown with a deliberate spiral twist in it, this being a popular boat people's fetish.

The great city of Reims, beyond, has been massacred in the cause of motorcar worship and the old port, which is silted up, lies alongside part of the maze of flyovers and

The Oise

itself has been formalized into a small park among the woods, with the sidings where the military trains were shunted in November 1918 picked out among the gravel. Here the representatives of the opposing forces met and Germany was vanquished. There is an inflammatory inscription in stone recording this event, and in a hall nearby a replica of the railway coach in which the signing took place. The original carriage was used in turn by Adolph Hitler to record the French capitulation of 1940 and after being taken to Berlin was destroyed in an air raid. Photographs are also on display showing the original rain-drenched scene in the forest, with a further series from the major battles. It is all most moving, but disturbing in that the lady who looks after the hall also sells Mars Bars as well.

Long vision is of near-vital importance on the Oise, as the locks are in pairs and the routes towards them divide a long way upstream. As the currents toward the weirs are often strong, the *péniches* and pusher tows that have begun to appear shut off power perhaps a mile upstream as they wait for the signal that a lock is ready. Once the way is clear they go like rockets, and it can be difficult to keep up. As all concerned rush for the lock entry it is possible to

a patient and sleek black cat with a white bow tie, and a very old duck, leaning forward on its faded yellow feet for all the world like an umpire in a village cricket match.

The Aisne used to be reported as 'sparkling', but alas blobs of foam now drift downstream from time to time, and the waters are not so sweet. The Oise, which follows, is a similar river but wider, and with even more traffic, which is saying something. There are stately towns such as Compiègne, l'Isle-Adam and Pontoise. All have quays, but to moor at the celebrated Armistice clearing upstream of Compiègne involves an uneasy liaison with branches, stones and the wash of passing craft. The Armistice site

Site of the Armistice, Compiègne. Marshal Foch looks down on the railway siding in a clearing near the Aisne.

hold intimate conversations with those about to overtake, as many craft have megaphones on the bow, with a switch in the wheelhouse.

Sometimes one lock is huge, the other tiny. At Verberie we found the big one out of order. A great jam of craft resulted and as many of the *péniches* on this river are equipped to push others, there were inevitable delays as these uncoupled. *Arthur* was trapped here for the night, and driven from his place by a vessel called *Dominique* which had tied to a tree that promptly bent double and shed all its branches under the strain. In the morning we took back our rightful place in the queue again and this we were accorded without question, despite a general fretting because of fog. Unless there is visibility of at least 300m traffic is not allowed to proceed on the rivers.

In times of flood, the weir barriers are sometimes lifted, and then, when a board with vertical green and white stripes is visible, it is possible to shoot through these giant sluices and to descend the river at a rapid pace. In normal circumstances the rectangular red and white striped 'no entry' board is hoisted to indicate that the weirs are in position. The current remains strong at all times, with these barrages often located close alongside the locks.

The pull of the weirs is fairly powerful. In heavy floods these barrages are sometimes lifted and craft may pass straight through.

The Aisne, Oise and Seine are all blue flag waterways, on which this symbol is displayed from the wheelhouse of an ascending vessel anxious to cheat the stream by taking the inside of a bend and passing contrary to the normal rule of the road. 'Keeping to the left' in this manner is a common practice on many of the larger Continental rivers. The skippers of upcoming craft call the tune, either by displaying the flag, flashing a light, or most commonly of all by pivoting into position a large blue board. Whether or not the ruling applies to pleasure craft is uncertain, but as there are frequent sections in which notices direct traffic to the 'wrong' side, and as these usually coincide with a glut of vessels, it is wise to fly the recognized signals in acknowledgement. The flag used is of a light 'electric' blue and about one metre square. Even then it can be difficult to see, particularly when a wind is blowing it horizontal, and it is for this reason that many captains prefer boards.

These same rivers are said to be 'free', so that even in the days of the *Permis de Circulation* none was theoretically needed by visitors to these waters. In practice lock-keepers are perpetually demanding *papiers*, usually so they can copy out names into record books, and unless one's French is good enough to argue it is wise to have some kind of ship's documents handy for display.

The Seine from Le Havre

Many British boats enter from the sea at Le Havre, as the quickest means of reaching the South of France from the English Channel by means of an inland route. Although that portion of the Seine between Le Havre and Conflans Ste-Honorine was not covered in *Arthur*, brief notes may be in order.

The great harbour of Le Havre can be entered at any state of tide, and there are yacht moorings inside the northern wall. As in all French Channel harbours, the greatest hazard is of being embroiled with an angler while manoeuvring, for lines are put out with great silliness from the piers high above.

As on all major rivers the traffic is vigorous and wash can be a problem. Stopping points are few, and advance planning is called for to avoid having to lie against a rough bank at nightfall.

In bad weather it is possible to bypass the worst part of the estuary by taking the 25km (16 mile) canal to Tancarville. This is a straight and dreary route, and really an extension of the docks. Entry from the outer harbour at Le Havre is by means of a small ship lock into the Bassin de la Citadelle. At the Tancarville end of the canal, almost beneath the mighty suspension bridge across the Seine, there is a further lock back into the river, open only near high water.

As an alternative to Le Havre, the charming little port of Honfleur may be preferred. There the dock gates open at about one hour before high water, which gives those leaving just sufficient time to find an anchorage in the sheltered part of the estuary before the ebb begins in earnest.

The River Seine is tidal as far as the first lock at Amfreville, 160km (100 miles) above Le Havre. In practice the tidal current decreases upriver, and upstream of Rouen, 120km (75 miles) from Le Havre, tidal calculation is not important. For craft ascending on the flood, as is customary, it is generally possible to reach Rouen on the one tide. There are just over eight hours in which to navigate upstream with the help of the current, but anyone possessed of *Reed's Nautical Almanac*, that essential volume for all seagoing boat owners, will be able to make their own more detailed calculations according to circumstance. High water at Rouen is five hours after that at Le Havre, and the flood begins at any point in the river three and a half hours beforehand.

After the refineries of Le Havre, the voyager passes for the larger part through peaceful countryside, with wooded hills as the river snakes this way and that. There are a few stopping points on the way, with walls or stagings, but below La Mailleraye, half way up to Rouen, care must be taken with the Mascaret, a tidal wave once lethal and still

Blue-flagging at Conflans-Ste-Honorine. The overtaking vessel
is a car transporter plying between factories on the Seine.

occasionally evident despite latterday improvements to
the river. In its prime, which appears to have been in the
mid-nineteenth century, the Mascaret was indeed an im-
mense wave, a wall of water sweeping the banks at Ville-
quier and Caudebec on the first of the incoming flood.
Today it appears only on spring tides, and takes the same
form as the bore on the River Trent, a sloping ramp of
water moving quite rapidly upstream, and although
occasionally breaking at the edges posing no great threat
to craft save in shallow water. Its arrival signifies an
immediate and total change in the direction of the current,
however, and with it comes a rapid rise in level. Any vessel

moored should accordingly be on very long lines and clear
of projections.

Those who have not cleared Customs at one of the
coastal ports may do so at Rouen, just after the first basin
on the port hand. There are several miles of good quay
beyond, and their presence should be relished, for there
are precious few other convenient moorings all the way up
to Paris.

There are four locks before the confluence with the
Oise. The character of these and of the navigation in
general is similar to that covered in greater detail on the
passage upstream of Conflans. Scenically the river is often
most dramatic, with limestone cliffs and the remnants of
castles overlooking the valley.

The Seine from Conflans-Ste-Honorine to Montereau

173km (107 miles) and 10 locks

Conflans is a boat people's town, with a floating church
among the hundreds of moored vessels that line the banks.
This is the junction of the Seine and Oise, a natural gathering point. Up the hill is a museum of inland navigation; all
around are the multifarious craft of the boating community. For the practical, there are fuel depots and
chandleries, where blue flags may be bought by those
impressed enough by the passing traffic to decide that they
need them.

In one hot afternoon *Arthur* pounded up from Conflans
to Île-St-Denis, just about the only other stopping point
before Paris itself. As hinted elsewhere, the river is remarkably unprovided with safe moorings, and as darkness sets
in and as the flow of barges of every size and shape con-

tinues unabated, the search for somewhere clear of a dangerous wash becomes a nightmare. It is every man for himself on the Seine, and anything not capable of at least six knots is among the walking wounded. The gravel *péniches* here have high-revving air-cooled diesels which wail like bandsaws, while heavy pusher convoys bully their way forward until a lock intervenes.

There are in fact several lock chambers at most of the sites. It is wise to hover, but with purpose, in order to see what the pattern is, and to claim one of the remaining spaces just inside the bottom gates. Occasionally there are garbled or hysterical interventions from loudspeakers, which add little except to the panic on board. Having been subjected to such a tirade at Bougival, the first lock up from Conflans, and then summoned to take our well-worn *papiers* to the control tower, I was amazed to find a most courteous and sympathetic lady in charge. The actual microphone work was undertaken by a gentleman sitting alongside who expressed no further comment upon my entry, merely sitting mute and gathering strength for the next apoplectic outburst; for, as I realized later, he shouted at everybody.

In these reaches the river stinks. There is a general aura of pollution while the banks – if they could but be reached – are often unsavoury. It was a relief to the crew of the *Arthur* to discover a line of pile stagings off the western shore of the Île-St-Denis, one of several spots where the stream divides. Lying alongside other craft is a useful resort in an emergency, though permission should always be asked out of courtesy and the adjoining decks scanned for ravenning hounds. The difficulty thus far had been in finding any such craft, for *péniches* as a species appeared either to be under way or down at Conflans-Ste-Honorine. Here, however, lay a useful assortment of vessels, for the larger part untenanted. After such a hunt, the fact that the stagings are in no way connected to the bank seems but a minor inconvenience. It is for such purposes that it is useful to carry planks.

Beyond, the traveller enters Paris, with one further ultra-modern lock at Suresnes. The entry of the city by water is an experience and a half, and it is tempting to say

Lock at Suresnes, Paris

that in bright sunlight there is little to compare. From the elegance of St-Cloud, right through the series of bridges to the mooring quays beside the Place de la Concorde, the river is superb. The burning of the palace of St-Cloud by the Prussians in 1870 is today rated an act of vandalism. The intention to pass a motorway along the river bank at Paris will perhaps be similarly regarded in years to come, but at the time of *Arthur*'s visit it had not yet been built.

There are many public quays in Paris, but those run by the Touring Club de France upstream of the Pont Alexandre III offer greater security. What can be more civilized than to lie in a boat at the centre of a great city, within a few moments' walk of its very heart?

In the evening the *bateaux mouches* skate by, spectacular floating conservatories, often equipped as restaurants, with rows of blazing headlights in defiance of every maritime convention. Pusher tugs drop their telescopic wheelhouses within split seconds of collision with the bridge and bring nearer the day when 2000 tons of cargo, bereft of its helmsman, will career onwards into the moorings on the bend. In the meantime it is merely choppy enough on the Seine for small boats to wobble like jellies in a whirlwind.

The Seine, looking downstream past the moorings of the
Touring Club de France

Pont Alexandre III, Paris

Notre Dame. There are one-way systems among the islands here.

The islands upstream offer further glories. A gracious short-term halt may made within the lee of Notre Dame. There are one-way systems on the river here, as there are through the arches of many of the bridges. When written down all these directions seem most complicated, but in practice it is merely necessary to follow the arrows and signal boards placed by the navigation authorities.

There are canals in Paris too, the St-Denis, St-Martin and the Canal de l'Ourq, originally constructed to supply water from a tributary of the Marne. All are interconnected and provide a means of navigating across the loop of the Seine; but they tend to be regarded warily, being administered independently by the City of Paris, with different provisos and regulations. With a lengthy underground section on the St-Martin, some swing bridges and several locks alongside roadways, they do not invite the casual traveller; nor, it is said, is he particularly welcome.

Upstream of Paris, and beyond the junction of the Marne, there is a rash of gravel pits and several apparently abandoned factories which upon closer examination prove to be working after all. Many miles of woodland then follow. Once again stopping places are in short supply, save at Melun, near the prison, or at the approaches to the locks, which are busy, if slow to operate. Some locks have recently been removed and the reaches deepened to accommodate the omnipresent pusher tugs. Of those chambers remaining, several are sloping sided, with slippery walls that pose problems of attachment and access. These also threaten propellers, while craft descending run the risk of becoming hooked up on some crevice as the water drops. From *Arthur* we would put crew ashore while skidding past the gates, leaving them clinging like gibbons to the rails. They could then run along the lockside to receive ropes.

Way upstream and beyond the Forest of Fontainebleau stands St-Mammès, another barge town, but a small one with a green right beside the water. From here runs a route to the south that is often held to be most convenient – by way of a sequence of canals that offers the smallest number of locks. The first of these is the Canal du Loing, and it is the River Loing which joins at St-Mammès.

The Seine may be followed much further upstream. Beyond Montereau it is known as La Petite Seine, and beyond Marcilly as La Haut-Seine, although here the stripling river is bypassed by a short canal which has progressively declined over the years. That final section is now navigable for a brief distance only.

Montereau is a big town with skyscraper blocks. Other travellers may care to visit the Routiers restaurant near the station – that is if they enjoy a meal accompanied by television, jukebox, the bellowing of lorry drivers, and table football played with such gusto that the legs leave the ground and the ball lands in people's soup. Rarely can one have the rich experience of someone shouting into one's ear at point-blank range, and of not being able to distinguish a single word, but I have sampled it here.

At Montereau the River Yonne runs in. As wide as the Seine at this point, the Yonne offers the first decent mooring for a very long time, on the eastern bank just above the confluence. It also forms part of other popular routes towards the south, by way of the Canal du Bourgogne or, for those with more time to spare, through the beautiful Canal du Nivernais, at the river's upstream end.

River Marne

197km (122 miles) and 22 locks, including portion of Canal Latéral à la Marne to the junction with Canal de l'Aisne à la Marne at Condé

A short way upstream of Notre-Dame the River Marne rather apologetically enters the Seine in surroundings of no great splendour. This is a further route that *Arthur* has been unable to take, thanks to a long-lasting conspiracy in the department that closes waterways for repairs, but the river should not be forgotten.

The Marne is another Thamesian waterway, once the suburbs of Paris have been left behind. There are numerous canalized sections and two short tunnels, one bypassing the bend at St-Maur and controlled by traffic lights, and the other upstream at Chalifert where it is every man for himself, although the lock-keepers will arbitrate in disputes. The locks themselves are substantially smaller than on the Seine.

The Marne is at the mercy of drought, and in 1971 the weirs were being supplemented with sandbags in order to sustain the modest but steady commercial traffic. It also suffers floods and then certain weir streams become the navigation channel and the locks may be bypassed. When ascending it is also possible to be misled by the eddies and to ram an abutment wall, as at least one *péniche* can testify, having stove in her anchors in so doing.

There is a cathedral at Meaux, and an old castle at Chateau-Thierry, where there are good moorings against the quay. It was at Chateau-Thierry that the last German offensive was checked by a combined French and American force in 1918, and driven back in the final push that forced the Armistice. The town has often been a centre of fighting and in 1814 was the scene of a Napoleonic victory.

The Marne becomes progressively more attractive as the voyager travels upstream, the long cuts being abandoned and the river winding through the Champagne country. Epernay, a centre of winemaking, stands at the head of navigation and effectively up a branch, for the straight Canal Latéral à la Marne diverts shortly before. The production of wine is visible to visitors, the premises of Moët et Chandon among others being open to public inspection by those who walk into the centre of Epernay and its Avenue de Champagne.

The Yonne

Yonne locks are large, and to close a far gate
the keeper has to walk a long way.

The sides are often sloping, and care must be
taken not to get caught up as the level drops.
Chambers of this type survive from the days
when narrow vertical walls were difficult to
build; the sloping form more easily resists
earth and water pressure.

L'Yonne

108km (67 miles) and 26 locks

For much of its length the River Yonne is wooded, with occasional towns on its long silvery reaches. Its weirs are real sparklers, tended in the main from pontoons that are winched across on the upstream side, so that the keepers may fiddle with the stick-like sluices and ponder on the Niagara of foam immediately below.

Like the Saône it is a fisherman's river, with the anglers seated in tranquility in small punts. They are there in the dusk and they are there in the early morning, bobbing gently in the mists like decoy ducks. There are few other bystanders, for the surroundings are largely rural.

Once again the locks are sloping sided, and vast, but unlike those of the Seine they are not electrified, and so it is easier to meet the keepers. The keeper of a lock on the Yonne tends to be deliberate in his movements, and he certainly doesn't come rushing out in an apron and a cloud of children, babbling apologies. Instead he walks with the measured tread of someone who knows that the route round to the opposite gate is a long, long way, and therefore demands some economy of effort. Often he wears a peaked cap with the initials of the Department of *Ponts*

Housing at Sens

of the Continental waterways. Barges carry it in large tonnages to other spots that seem to have gravel of their own anyway, while lock-keepers treat it reverently, grading and raking it on their paths, with an enthusiasm inversely proportional to the other work that they have to do.

There is little traffic on the Yonne, except in the grain season, which starts in mid-July and builds to a crescendo in the early autumn. There may then be long waits at the locks, for a man who has just set the gates for a downcomer is not likely to leap into action when some upstream traveller heaves into sight first. And since the locks can take many craft, the chamber may well be held in readiness until several have appeared.

By contrast with the long walks and the cumbersome winding of the gates, many of the *vannes* are operated by simple levers which lift or drop slotted shutters within the gates. Like all sluice systems these must be treated with caution for, once released, the levers can fly over on their own with some force.

Having seen a *péniche* get hung up on a lockside, I can report that the signal on such occasions is a series of blasts on the ship's siren, whereupon much frantic operation of the *vannes* takes place. For those fearful of damage to propellers, the best bet is to lie, if possible, between the vertical abutments that support the gates.

Traffic does not continue at night, while the banks are often soft, so that mooring is seldom a problem. There are otherwise quays at Sens, at Villeneuve, a symmetrical town with turreted gateways, and at Joigny.

The railway is close at hand for much of the way, but finally crosses over at Laroche to harass the Canal de Bourgogne which here branches off to the east. The Yonne then continues through long cuts or *dérivations* and some pleasant further reaches before the town of Auxerre.

Auxerre, pronounced 'O-ssair', is splendidly located on a hill beside the river, dominated by the cathedral of Saint-Etienne. The narrow streets of the old city are delightful, while the river frontage illustrates a happy civic attitude towards the water. Municipal moorings have now been provided on the east bank, but the town side is just as good.

et Chaussées embroidered upon it. Frequently he loves his gravel, which he rakes endlessly and which he takes a dim view of people like the crew of the *Arthur* cavorting about on. Indeed, gravel is a major factor in the running

Auxerre. Upstream of the city the river forms part of the Canal du Nivernais.

Secunda, high up the Nivernais (*Sandra Cumming*).

A Navigational Note

Since first publication of this book, I have exchanged the *Arthur* for *Secunda*, a Dutch *klipper*, now converted as a *hotel-péniche* carrying ten guests. A detailed account of *Secunda*'s acquisition (and the Netherlands waterways) may be found in the companion volume *Barge Country*, and I have subsequently travelled both the Nivernais and the Yonne many times each season. Some further navigational points may be made, as follows.

In times of flood, even in summer, the Yonne is a transformed waterway. There is a strong set under the bridges, and the safest course, if descending, is to let a vessel gently through the nearside arch, with a line from a bollard on the bank. This particularly applies to the Pont Paul Bert at Auxerre, and at Joigny, where the current in the other arches carries the unwary into the abutments. If voyaging in the other direction, care must be taken to approach each lock near the bank, but at an angle, to overcome the circular eddy formed by the weir, which will at the last moment carry one away towards the weirstream.

Higher up the Canal du Nivernais, the problems are more of depth, although there is a tricky river crossing at Basseville, not far short of Clamecy. Here a strong sideways current compels a tortuous passage into the lock. If in a heavy vessel ignore all advice on crossing quickly, for none of these good people have any experience in stopping again in the short space that is available.

In the canal sections higher up, water levels can still vary daily, through leaks in the night, combined with a *laissez-faire* attitude. I now always send an advance party to parley and coerce at the very first symptoms.

Canal du Nivernais

174km (108 miles) and 114 locks

To enter this waterway is to step back in time, to gentleness and relaxation. It is possibly the most beautiful French canal of all, almost certainly the most varied. My small nieces were aboard *Arthur* when we entered from Auxerre; a lady lock-keeper gave them walnuts, another cut flowers from her garden. It is that sort of an area.

For many miles the River Yonne still winds in and out, twinkling at its weirs, cool and turquoise under the hillsides. There is virtually no commercial traffic, save over a short distance during the grain season, so that it is possible to moor almost anywhere. There are frequent sleepy villages, and the odd small town, such as Cravant where I have witnessed a public celebration such as takes place on Bastille Day and other *jours de fête*. A small band

Lock-keeper on the Nivernais (*Hugh McKnight*)

Statue to the *flotteurs*, founders of the navigation, on the bridge at Clamecy

plays, without discernible rhythm, from a platform draped with the tricolour in front of the town hall. Citizens dance in the sloping square with an admirable disregard for passing traffic, while youths and tiny tots light thunder-flashes in their midst. From a table around the corner the gendarmerie will provide free red wine for anyone who asks for it.

Cravant is a tiny walled town surrounded by cornfields, from which there are excellent views up the canyon of the Yonne. Even more spectacular are the cliffs of Saussois further upstream, rising vertically from near the water's edge. Here rock climbing is practised, but a path provides an easier way to the top.

Although the full link between the Yonne and Loire was not completed until 1842, that part in the Yonne valley was used much earlier, and before any locks were ever built, as a means of floating timber down to Paris. A statue near the lock at Clamecy credits Jean Rouvet with starting the process in the mid-sixteenth century, while another on the town bridge itself commemorates the *flotteurs*, the lumbermen who laid the foundations of Clamecy's prosperity. The gentleman depicted has a

The rocks of Le Saussois, twenty miles upstream of Auxerre

Dirol, a typical small village on the ascent above Clamecy.
Lift bridges are worked by keepers going ahead by autocycle.

over the smouldering piles of wood and earth. It looked, in the sunlight, quite a satisfying occupation.

The higher levels are all of artificial canal, although the river still runs close until the final climb up through dense woods to the summit at Port Brulé. This uppermost section of the Nivernais has never been modernized to the standards of the Freycinet Act, and its locks are slightly shorter. It is for this reason that the canal carries little commercial traffic, for it no longer provides a through route. The occasional *péniche* struggles up to a silo at one or other of the villages down by the Yonne, but with difficulty, for the canal is now badly silted.

For several years the Nivernais was in danger of closure. The gates leaked, the stonework crumbled; there was no longer any cause for a tug through the three cool tunnels at the top, or the narrow cuttings in between. In the nick of time the Saint Line hire company moved there from the Marne in the mid-1960s and established a base beside the lake at Baye, just beyond the third of the tunnels. Today the pleasure boat traffic has increased, a certain amount of maintenance work has been done, and the threatened section has passed into the hands of the local authorities, who provide the necessary finance. But un-

peaked cap and baggy trousers which, in the manner of so much French statuary, appear to be moulded out of dough. Today Clamecy no longer floats the timber from the woods around but has instead factories devoted to the production of carbon. With the exception of a gravel quarry higher up this is the only industrial outcrop on the whole of the Nivernais, and it may be bypassed altogether by taking a loop of the Yonne instead of the straight canal that runs past the coolers and hissing pipes. As compensation for the demise of the raftmen, I have seen in the woods up above a charcoal burner of the Arthur Ransome variety, black-faced and grimacing

Lockhouse on the final climb to Port Brulé

Entering the narrows between tunnels on the summit
near Baye. A tug once plied here, but now no commercial
traffic ever passes.

Plates at each lock cottage list name and
number. Those on the other side of the
watershed give numbers towards the Loire.

doubtedly the Nivernais stayed open at a critical time
because of Saint Line's action, and later generations
will be grateful.

The twin lakes of Baye and Vaux both provide water for
the canal, but in the odd and complex way of inland
systems, they feed into the southern portion of the
Nivernais only. For, although the summit level of the
canal flows right alongside the beautiful lake at Baye, it
is a few feet higher. Water for canals is often procured
with difficulty, nor is it to be squandered, particularly
if there has been little rain or snowfall in the winter.
Prior to *Arthur*'s visit, there had been three successive
dry winters, and as a result the neighbouring Canal du
Bourgogne and the Canal de la Marne à la Saône had both
suffered closures during the following summers. Thus

The lake at Baye, one of two which also serve as reservoirs.
The canal is separated by the wall, and stands at a slightly
higher level.

the larger the number of reservoirs for storage the better. The Nivernais has three, the last being at a lake several miles distant and flowing by way of a lofty aqueduct at Montreuillon. It is possible to take a small dinghy to the head of this stream and be borne down on the current until the joining point at Port Brulé (a tiny hamlet in the woods); but it was never intended as a navigation, merely as one of the subsidiary works that are necessary on even the humblest of canals.

On the southern side the Nivernais changes again, with more open countryside, the occasional small château or turreted farmhouse, and one or two further river sections,

this time embracing the twisting River Aron. Châtillon-en-Bazois, Cercy-la-Tour and Decize are the only towns.

There are few practical points to add, since this is a beginner's waterway, without the pressures of the Seine or Oise. The equipment varies enormously, being the makeshift remains of many other routes, but the keepers are quite amenable, and if the *vannes* should be wound down, rather than up, in order to let the water in, they will quite happily explain. It is worth noting, however, that keepers sometimes work several locks or lift-bridges, not necessarily in consecutive order, since *madame* at lock number 4 may quite happily turn out to do her stint, while a more active gentleman whizzes from 1, 2 and 3 and then on to number 5 on his bike. When the canal was threatened the lock-keepers were glad to see any boat, for their livelihood and attractive cottages were all at stake. Now there is a tendency to whirl the voyager onwards, in order to get rid of him, and the practice of telephoning ahead does not help, as the next lock is always ready, and the keeper waiting to pass a boat through *poste haste*. Such is human nature; it is wise in these circumstances to take it easy around lunchtime, lest by luring a canal employee far from home you starve him in the course of duty. It helps also to make plain one's intentions of stopping and to be firm about it, whatever terrible stories are told of gout, chronic inability to work the next day, or the tendency of a particular section to run dry during the night.

The canal joins the River Loire at Decize, and this must be crossed, provided it is not in flood, when the lock-keeper will not let you. The old chain tug stands idle and apparently abandoned (although this is difficult to be sure of in France). In lieu of its services, the voyager is now presented with a tiny map by the last keeper on the Nivernais in order that he may distinguish the main course of the Loire from several tributaries and side streams. After about a kilometre another lock, with elegant cast iron gates, gives access to a basin of the Canal Latéral a la Loire, which runs parallel to the river on the other side.

The Loire itself is no longer navigable for most of its course, although centuries ago boats were floated down it

Châtillon-en-Bazois

Animal haulage on the Loire near Decize, perhaps the last
such sight in France. The driver signals to his charges by
tapping on the towline with his stick.

Passing on a tight section. Both crews took it slowly, and
stirred up the mud.

the barge glided down on the current, then, responding
to a tap with a stick on the towline, they would lunge
forwards for a moment in order to arrest the vessel's progress and turn it into the lock. As by official decree all
haulage using 'animals' has been forbidden on the canals
themselves, this was possibly the last such sight in France.

Loing, Briare, Latéral à la Loire and Centre

410km (255 miles) and 150 locks

An alternative route off the Seine may be taken at St-
Mammès and through the chain of four canals listed
above. This is the track often followed by those bent on
reaching the Mediterranean, since, on balance, it is held to
offer the shortest journey time. On the way it passes
Decize and the junction with the Canal du Nivernais
described in the previous chapter.

It is a route detested by the majority of working boat
people for its lack of maintenance and extreme shallowness
by commercial standards. Nonetheless many *péniches* are
compelled to use it, and until the day when the official
notice at St-Mammès can be removed many delays may be
expected due to commercial craft hogging the channel.
The notice states that loaded depth must be limited to
1.80m, whereas many *péniches* are designed to draw 2.00m
or 2.20m. Needless to say each captain carries as much as
he dares, and it is held that the repair yards at either end
do a steady business in repairing worn out bottoms. There
is much luck in the matter of encountering other traffic,
but those impatient for the fleshpots of the south must be
prepared for delays.

The Canal du Loing skirts the Forest of Fontainebleau,
and whatever the mutterings of the barge people, it can be

and then burned at journey's end (or alternatively dis-
mantled and brought back on carts; the stories vary).
The current and shallows, found in all save a state of
flood, defeat ordinary navigation and, although President
de Gaulle strongly supported a plan to modernize the
Loire on the lines of the Rhine, this has never taken place
and journeys downstream are rarely practicable.

Until a year or so after my visits in the *Arthur*, the
Loire at Decize offered a unique spectacle, for donkeys
were still being used to draw laden sand barges from a
dredger out in the stream. Working in tandem, and
harnessed to a yoke, they would trot obediently ahead as

The aqueduct at Briare, built by Eiffel in the 1890s. Prior to its construction craft worked through locks down into the Loire, then climbed again to the Latéral canal on the other side.

quite spectacular. In pouring rain the surrounding pines take on an eerie steaming quality, and there are picturesque houses and watermills. Sisley painted the canal, and Delius lived close by at Grez, now adjacent to the motorway crossing. Nemours, just beyond, provides a pleasant mooring in the Loing itself, which for a short distance participates in the navigation.

The Canal de Briare follows, and this was the first major canal in Europe. The Chinese had already built canals, and the first chambered lock is reputed to have been constructed there in the tenth century AD. Leonardo da Vinci invented mitring gates, and there had been a number of river navigations incorporating locks of various sorts,

but the Briare, opened in 1642, can be adjudged the first canal of the type we know today. It was 34 miles long and had 41 locks. It connected the Loire with the Loing, and effectively the Seine, although all these rivers were relatively uncertain navigations. Near the town of Montargis, at the start of the Briare, the remnants may be seen of the Canal d'Orleans which was built not long after, and this was the canal that Forester remarked upon in *The Motor Boat* of 1928. He found that it smelled and was pleased to lock through into the Loire, where he and his wife experienced little trouble, as the *Annie Marble* drew four inches only and was light enough to be heaved over the sandbanks. The Foresters journeyed 300 miles to the port of Nantes, past 'golden sands and blue water and towering cliffs and green hills'. It was, he said, 'intensely solitary'.

The Canal d'Orleans was effectively closed to navigation in 1954, its locks never having been improved to the general standard. On the Briare some traces of this earlier vintage may also be seen, for the original line of the canal is sometimes visible, particularly at the town of Rogny, where the masonry of an old seven-lock staircase is preserved as a monument. Hughes Cosnier, the architect of the Briare, is certainly worth commemoration, and had his sponsor Henry IV not died his canal might have been finished even earlier, for by 1611, seven years after work had begun, the canal was almost complete. Cosnier himself died before the Canal de Briare was opened, but is generally considered its engineer.

Briare itself is a little town beside the Loire, and an iron aqueduct, built by Eiffel in the 1890s, now carries craft above the river. Grand and imposing, it measures 660m overall, with ornamental columns at each end and twirly cast iron lamp standards above its paths. It provides a suitable finale to an attractive waterway and marks a change from a wooded, gently hilly landscape to the plains of the upper Loire.

The portion of the Loire in which the celebrated *châteaux* are placed, and providing something of a touristic surfeit, is further west, toward the sea. The Canal Latéral à la Loire runs in the opposite direction, through lonesome countryside. At Châtillon-sur-Loire a short

The Latéral à la Loire. An arm near Sancerre.

walk reveals the waiting basins and hauling causeway out in the river, from which craft were winched before the Briare aqueduct was built. The old lockhouse here, high above the floodline, is an atmospheric beauty, likewise the occasional village further on, to be sought out by bicycle in the tracery of byroads towards the west. The wine centre of Sancerre offers the only hills prominent from the canal, which runs in straight-line jags with shallow, uncomplicated locks at regular intervals.

At its halfway point, the deceptive Latéral links with a remnant of one of the most romantic waterways of all. This was the Canal du Berry, which ran off in erratic Y formation into some of the quietest and most beautiful countryside in France. Built in the 1820s, for the larger

part by Spanish prisoners of war, it incorporated many locks and five aqueducts. One arm ran south to Montluçon. The other straggled northwest through Bourges and into the valley of the Cher, the remote and atmospheric region that forms the background to Alain-Fournier's *Le Grand Meaulnes*, now published by Penguin and the subject of a strange but remarkable film 'The Wanderer'.

The Berry Canal was narrow, and being built through limestone it leaked badly. Everything was tried, from pumps to the creation of extra reservoirs, and then to the final counsel of despair, a reduction in the navigable level. Finally, in 1954, the Canal du Berry was closed. Some of the *berrichons*, the unique craft of the region, moved out onto the main line of the Latéral at the junction, the old canal town of Marseilles-lès-Aubigny. When I passed through in 1967 several were still there, sunk; others were lived on as houseboats by canal people in

The last of the *berrichons* in 1967. These craft measured 28 by 2.70 metres (91ft by 8ft 10in) and carried up to 100 tons. (*Hugh McKnight*)

retirement; and one was still working, carrying cement and drawn by a mule and a donkey. The *berrichons* looked not unlike the English narrow boat, and if fractionally bigger were even more spartan. The animals were housed aboard in a stable amidships, while the family which manned each boat lived under a tent on the stern. When fully laden, a *berrichon* moved at just over one knot, with first one animal straining forward and then the other as they tugged against a wooden yoke which gave them a purchase against the load of the boat.

There were other horse-drawn boats at that time, mostly of a type fractionally smaller than a *péniche*, and if anything even slower than a *berrichon*. They were known, perhaps appropriately, as *bâtards*, for they constituted a terrible stumbling block to all other traffic as they staggered up the cut, barely moving and taking an eternity at the locks.

I once had the opportunity of studying them all in detail at a place called le Guétin, where the Latéral crosses the River Allier by an aqueduct preceded by two staircase locks. There had been, quite inevitably, a *chômage*, a stoppage for repairs, and the traffic had built up the

Cast iron gates at the basin near Decize

Towing tractor at Le Guétin. The owner of the *berrichon* stands in peaked cap and checked shirt among a group of boatmen from Belgium and the Netherlands.

customary queue of the stoical and the infuriated. But at staircase locks the system is even more complicated than normal, because the lock chambers directly connect. Because of this it is more efficient for all traffic to proceed in one direction, and to meet such a situation there tend to be blanket regulations in France. The locks were used for descending vessels in the mornings, and for ascending craft in the afternoons, which was fine until the balance

Crossing the Loire again, at Digoin

of traffic became uneven. I was once at Le Guétin in such a situation, with fifteen vessels waiting to climb the staircase but not being allowed to because it was not their time of day. The aqueduct is an extra complication at this point, for while a vessel is upon it the upper lock chamber cannot be filled, lest the craft be drawn back by the water flowing down the tight channel. Horses, mules and donkeys were not permitted to cross the aqueduct at all, as it was considered too dangerous, so they were sent around by the road bridge instead, to mingle with the passing Citroens and Berliets. In the meantime a terrible old tractor would be produced from out of a derelict shed, and after much gasping and shuddering, this would drag the *berrichon* or the occasional *bâtard* across to the other side, watched by a seething mob from the Low Countries. Le Guétin is a name to conjure with.

By the time *Arthur* appeared on the scene all horse-drawn craft had been banned from the Latéral, and the luckless families who could not afford to motorize were compelled to give up, lying at such points as the old arm down to Nevers, or at Digoin where the Loire is crossed again by another lock-and-aqueduct combination at the

Montceau-les-Mines

Automatic lock equipment on the Canal du
Centre. A pull on the right-hand cord sets gates
and paddles into action. The left-hand string
stops everything in emergency.

start of the next waterway in the line, the Canal du
Centre.

This is a grim old canal, with that certain atmosphere of
decay that characterizes all colliery areas. At the town of
Montceau-les-Mines, for many years now a Polish settle-
ment, the largest colliery loading bay is now closed and
abandoned, while another handles only a desultory traffic.
The great basin, until recently thronged with craft, now
contains perhaps two motor *péniches* briefly stopping on
their journey to the south. There is a monument here to
a mining disaster, to which plaques have been added as
other dreadful accidents have followed. It was to this point
that the majority of the old horse-drawn vessels once
plied.

Haulage with animals was quite exciting in the later
days for the towpath also did duty as a Route Nationale,
which runs close alongside for much of the way, and as
the Canal du Centre winds much more than the Latéral
there must have been a number of surprises.

Nearby is the celebrated ironworking town of Le
Creusot, established after the Englishman William
Wilkinson had built the first coke furnace at this point.
Thereafter the Centre improves a little, with pleasant if
undistinguished countryside spiced with the odd reminder
of the labours on which we all depend, as the odd factory
toils on or a miners' bus splashes up the road in the early
dawn.

The Saône at Chalon

It is at such spots that captains on the alert can renew their supplies of bottled gas, for plaques appear by the waterside from time to time, advertising this brand or that. I exchanged ours at the village of St-Leger, after a brisk canter among the mongrels in a back garden where bottles could be exchanged. Such opportunities arise perhaps once every second day, short of staggering off to some faraway town with a gas bottle tied to the bicycle. The wise mariner, of course, keeps a spare container as a refill and can then afford to wait a day or so until an exchange centre passes close at hand.

At Chalon-sur-Saône a final and extremely deep lock gives access to the river. Chalon, itself a thriving centre in Roman times, prospered with the coming of the canal in the later eighteenth century, and the ramparts and quays on the riverside were built by Emiland Gauthey, the engineer of the Centre. Today a new cut has been built to bypass the old section that once ran into the middle of the town and it is through this, and the quite appalling effluent it contains, that the voyager can greet the Saône.

Canal de Bourgogne

242km (150 miles) and 189 locks

Arthur had to wait until his second year in France before attempting this well known and spectacular track to the 'Côte d'Or'. Our previous plan to cross by this route had been frustrated by lack of water. The Bourgogne often suffers in this manner, particularly in late summer, when the tendency is to close the summit level first and then successive reaches lower down, culminating with the section between Dijon and the Saône, the only portion carrying a heavy traffic.

The Bourgogne is one of two canals (the other being the Marne à la Saône) on which we found the locks to be closed on Sundays, on the somewhat mysterious grounds that as the canal is not very busy anyway, the lock-keepers

The spirit of decay assumes a greater charm on the final descent to the Saône. Nor is it really dispelled by the automatic locks, the only properly functioning type that *Arthur* had yet encountered. Sensing eyes detect oncoming craft and prepare a flight accordingly. Once in a lock it is merely necessary to pull a string and the whole thing works on its own accord (although an emergency string is provided lest it does not). Water rushes in, or out, and the gates open. Floating bollards are also provided, and even if the coal closures have cut the traffic, modernization of the remaining locks is continuing. Of some extra interest on this lazy descent is the tilemaking township of St-Julien-sur-Dheune, where the roofs of the houses are brightly patterned in different colours, rather in the manner of a Fair Isle sweater.

A lock on the Bourgogne. Wood is kept stacked for the winter.

The château at Tanlay, near Tonnerre, constructed in the
sixteenth and seventeenth centuries

require a rest. I fully sympathize with them, and would
be quite happy to work the locks on my own, but such
thoughts engender a dumb-struck horror, and it is the
fashion instead for both boat crews and keepers to spend
the day idling.

There are many, many locks, but some consoling views,
with a constant change of scene. Almost throughout its
length the Canal de Bourgogne is lined with trees, first
of all as long straight avenues, and then as the main line
railway is left behind, in swirling bends up into the hills.
There are also numerous villages and small towns:
St-Florentin, standing spikily up on a mound; Tonnerre
where the fit and agile can clamber up to the church and
perhaps like the crew of *Arthur* hear modern jazz played
rather too seriously as part of a cultural series organized
throughout Burgundy.

There are *châteaux* too, including a magnificent one at
Tanlay, close by the canal. I walked into the grounds one
morning as the mists lifted. A man was mowing the grass,
two children ran out to play, a nun came by to feed the
goldfish. The noisy streets of London seemed spiritually
a long way off.

As the canal climbs further the hillsides close in a
little, grey-green in the morning light but not overpower-
ing, as the locks follow in rapid succession. There is a
saying among the boat people of 'he holds the valley',
and indeed for anyone behind a loaded boat there are
few opportunities of getting past. But commercial craft
are a rarity on the upper levels. There is, say, one a day
on average, and that one could well be travelling in the
opposite direction.

In the various debates on which canal route across
France is the most convenient, the Bourgogne is sometimes supported as being scenically enticing, which is
correct, and as having easily operated locks, which is
odd. In general principle they are the same as anywhere
else, although the gates are opened by leaning on a steel
lever arm, somewhat like the handle of a plough. But the
large *vannes* tend to be mysterious, being housed somewhere in the ground beneath cast iron pedestals. The
upstream pedestal lets water into the lock; that downstream bypasses it. The only indication as to whether
they are open or shut is a little disc that rotates in the
ground, moving through a quarter circle from F for
fermé to O for *ouverte*, though sometimes vice versa and
occasionally part way in between. Local advice on the
matter can be colourful, and if in doubt it is best left to the
experts; in any event winding these *vannes de terre* seems
to be the lock-keeper's prerogative. There is also a strange
system of leaving the gate *vannes* part open, in order to
run water down to the lower reaches, all of which seems
most improvident in view of the Bourgogne's usual
troubles.

By and large the keepers here are a cheery race, with
the time to devote to their smallholdings and other secon-

Cutting on the summit level at Pouilly

Motorway to the south, near Pouilly-en-Auxois.
The canal lies beyond the trees in the
background.

dary businesses. Vegetables and fowl may be readily purchased, but if the latter, it comes as a small surprise to find that the bird is still alive and merely suspended by its feet. For a small consideration *madame* will readily slaughter any hen (it is well not to look at this point for the French method is far from neat), and pluck it.

In its final ascent to the summit the canal shares the valley with the motorway to the south. The continuous roar of all motorways reverberates across the valley as a constant succession of caravans and trucks howls abruptly past the front door of a country house that has wisely been deserted. By contrast the canal seems very much of another world, and a pleasant one to return to, after a stroll to gaze down the new highway that streaks like an arrow

towards the horizon. A surprising number of the motorists passing by are British.

At the summit is a tunnel 3347m long, running beneath the small tourist town of Pouilly-en-Auxois. By French standards it is extremely low, and it is because of this that commercial traffic is so slight. Empty *péniches* arriving are laboriously put into a tank, which is itself then partially sunk prior to being towed through by the electric tug. The electric wires themselves are also lower than elsewhere, and although 'yachts' are frequently allowed to pass through under their own steam, there is some doubt as to whether the current is left switched on at the time. But as the tunnel too is closed on Sundays, *Arthur* moored in the basin at Pouilly, and the crew walked a few kilometres to the nearby village games.

These were advertised as being on Sunday the 28th of July, although the 28th was in fact a Saturday. But as the proprietor of the restaurant explained, the poster was just a minor mistake and everyone knew it all took place on a Sunday anyway. The games themselves were good rustic stuff – walking across water on a greasy pole, pillow

Village games at Arconcay

cables, a source of worry on any vessel with a high super-structure, tend to sag even further *beyond* the tunnel, and this may not be noticed in the general euphoria of emerging.

At Vandernesse another château stands high on the horizon, and is worth a walk, even on a Tuesday when most public buildings in France are shut, for there are splendid views and some shops. I was tickled to find that by the château old postcards were on sale at two francs each (including one of Stoke-on-Trent, taken in the 1920s) whereas in a shop near the canal cards of a similar vintage could be acquired for 35 centimes, with the proprietress apologizing that they were so old. The canal shop also had, and by all normal laws still has, a staggering pile of shoes, a monument to reckless buying, a positive lorry load, all in a heap on the storeroom floor.

After Vandernesse and tiny Pont d'Ouche the motor-way closes in again. There follows a suburb of Dijon, in which the valley has been imaginatively flooded to create a water recreation area around the new tower blocks and estates. Dijon itself, the gastronomic centre of France, sports all the fine buildings but few cheap restaurants. An

fights, being rolled across the field inside a tractor tyre, and so on. The village of Arconçay defeated the village of Magnien in practically every event, having roughly four times the population to choose from. Each team had one pretty girl who inevitably got thrown in and the grand-stand was on a haycart. On the way we looked at the old horse path over the tunnel marked by ventilation shafts, and into the tranquil church at Choisy-le-Désert, another tiny village typical of the many all around.

There had been further celebrations at Vandernesse, just beyond the tunnel, and if there is any advice to proffer to voyagers on the Bourgogne it is to watch the posters closely, for such functions should not be missed. We ar-rived in time to witness the packing up of the stalls, having dallied on the journey through the tunnel. The technical should note that both portals are considerably larger than the bore within, as the brickwork drops suddenly a few feet inside each entrance. Furthermore, the overhead

Vandernesse, near Dijon

Southeastern portal
of the tunnel.
Just inside the roof
level drops sharply.

expensive one is worth visiting, however, while coach
tours may be taken around the vineyards to the south,
with *son et lumiére* provided and judicious sampling allowed towards the end of the journey.

It was at Dijon that the first experiments were made in
electric haulage for canal craft, using current generated
from the flow of water at one of the locks. From this ex-
periment, conducted in 1892, the electric mule developed,
first as a tricycle running on pneumatic tyres, then later
on rails. Bank towage persisted on this particular section
until very recently, for there is a steady traffic in gravel
from the Saône, but in its last years diesel tractors appear
to have been used.

From the large basin at Dijon to the boatmen's town of
St-Jean-de-Losne the canal runs dead straight all the way,
a distance of over sixteen miles. There are attractive lock
houses with fading green paint, and a certain taste of the
South. More lofty trees mark this long section out into the
plain and despite its straightness it is most impressive.

St-Jean-de-Losne has a large basin which provides a
good spot to lie, and for lovers of local colour a café
straight out of Simenon, where you do not need a cigarette
in your mouth in order to enjoy the smoke. There are more
elegant establishments beside the river, and also a bridge,
where a monument commemorates the town's successful
defence in 1636 with a handful of troops against an army
of the Holy Roman Empire. Today there are gatherings of
barge people at St-Jean, for it is very much a boatman's
town, with occasional galas and handling competitions
among the *péniches*.

The Saône

Péniches at St-Jean-de-Losne

Canal de la Marne à la Saône
224km (139 miles) and 114 locks

The Canal de la Marne à la Saône is sometimes chosen by virtue of its light traffic, agreeable scenery, and sandy and comparatively hospitable bottom. This is another waterway where entry in *Arthur* was thwarted. A *chômage*, totally unscheduled, by a matter of minutes prevented us from entering from the Saône in 1973. The previous lock-keeper had not been told, and thus failed to convey the necessity of reaching the entrance by a certain deadline.

I can claim to know part of this canal quite well, having walked many miles of towpath looking for a non-existent boat. There is a certain irony in paying about £7 for a taxi and then being obliged to sleep under a tree in the middle of nowhere. The moral is to have a contingency plan, so that if you are called away from the boat, as I was, you can follow a certain course when it proves not to have reached the rendezvous agreed. As a sideline, I can recommend sleeping in deep countryside in rural France—provided it does not rain. And when a message has finally been received, in the very early morning, when lock-keepers are once again awake and amenable to enquiry, hitch-hiking is fairly easy, for there is a certain bond between all men who are up at dawn.

The Marne à la Saône was cut surprisingly recently, being finished only in 1907. Like the Canal de l'Est, it ascends to well over 1000ft above sea level. Here the 4820m Souterrain de Balesmes necessitates towing to an uncertain schedule, and local enquiry is advised. There are several small townships on the way, principal among them being Chaumont beside the infant River Marne. There are pleasant woodlands, one or two interesting bends to steer around, and a tendency for the lock-keepers to inveigle passing tourists into drunken social gatherings. The locks are hand-winders, and as on the Canal de Bourgogne they are closed on Sundays.

The Saône and the Rhône
St-Symphorien to the Mediterranean, 547km (340 miles) and 20 locks

Broad and, occasionally interesting still, the Saône flows on. St-Jean-de-Losne, the bargemen's town, and the ramparts of Chalon both offer moorings, but much of the section between them has now been converted into a boring dyke that cuts across many of the river's more attractive loops. A number of locks have been spirited away also, in the interest of easier if not particularly stimulating navigation.

As the Saône descends towards Lyon it becomes quirky in the matter of depth, and worried barge people sometimes seek out pilots. The average 'yacht' has little need of their services, but crews may prefer to carry the *Carte de la Saône de Lyon â St-Jean-de-Losne*, available in Chalons or at a floating shop and fuel depot at St-Jean itself. There are underwater groynes and walls in places and it pays not to shy too far from the path of upcoming barges lest these be struck. Alternatively a book, *Guide de la Saône*, may be aquired and the traveller can then breeze down to Lyon by way of Tournus, Mâcon and the pleasant town of Trevoux. If the river is in flood the journey may be accelerated by passing down each weir stream, but it is wise to consult the traffic signs before so doing. An arrow will point the way, while a green and white horizontal board indicates which portion of a weir may be shot. For those with time to spare, the short but beautiful River Seille, which joins just below Tournus, well merits exploration.

The city of Lyon, the third largest in France, offers many sights, from the Roman onwards, and by ascending the basilica on the hill of Fouvière it is possible to see it all, and allegedly Mont Blanc 100 miles to the east.

The Port de Plaissance at Lyon is by the Pont Napoleon. There are excellent facilities for the travel-weary, and an

Lyon: the Port de Plaisance (*Nicholas Hopkinson*)

opportunity to ponder before being swept off by the River Rhône, which joins just around the next corner.

The Rhône has a reputation as a helter-skelter. There are tales of yachts whistling down sideways and backwards on the swirling current and of craft disintegrating upon impact with the stones beneath the famous half-bridge at Avignon.

Certainly when I first saw it in 1960 this was a very rapid river indeed; at the time of *Arthur*'s visit it was still too fast for a return trip upstream, and for this reason we did not go. But the Rhône is a river in transition, being modified and improved rather on the lines of the Grand Canal d'Alsace. With work now authorized on the Rhine-Saône link it will ultimately become a very busy waterway indeed, supplying bulk materials to and from the industrial developments of the south.

This work has now been completed and the river is largely tamed, although it remains fairly swift by British standards and a fair chop may be generated on some of the long, exposed reaches. Pilots are no longer necessary, although a pocket guide or map may be of value, a small expense by comparison with the exorbitant fees that pilots used to charge. In 1973 a pilot cost between thirty and forty pounds for the passage between Lyon and Arles, despite having to do virtually nothing except eat and drink the ship's supplies and demonstrate a little local knowledge over the two short sections at either end of that journey, which were still awaiting improvement. It is ironic that in the real days of pilotage, when the river was a rock-infested torrent, the fees were said to be modest.

A strip map, the *Carte Guide du Rhône de Lyon à la Mer* by Henri Vagnon, can be obtained in shops at Lyon or at the navigation offices downstream and across the river from the Port de Plaisance. The channel is marked, and with common sense the river can normally be navigated without undue stress. This is, incidentally, another blue flag waterway and as the amount of traffic is ever-growing it will pay the prudent to invest in one of these signals and follow the same procedures as on the Aisne, Oise or Seine. At the time of writing, night navigation is prohibited.

The speed of the current varies, depending upon rain or snow in the mountains and upper valleys. At its fastest it perhaps reaches six or seven knots over short distances, and therein lies the difficulty for small craft wishing to return. Towage can be negotiated at a price, but the fast *petroliers* and other commercial craft which ply will want to do so at their normal pace, and the safe speed at which any vessel may travel, expressed in knots, is slightly below the square root of twice her waterline length, in feet. Thus *Arthur*, measuring 54ft on the waterline, can travel at no more than the square root of 108, giving a limiting speed of 10 knots. A boat of only 25ft on the waterline will be limited to less than 7 knots, unless

L'Ecluse André Blondel at St-Pierre-de-Bollène. A hydroelectric station stands alongside. (*Nicholas Hopkinson*).

she can 'plane', that is rise partially out of the water. Not all tugs are willing to travel so slowly and it is for such reasons that so many small boats in distress at sea disintegrate upon being given a tow by a passing ship.

Thus the various alternatives on the Rhône, until its final modernization, are to seek a considerate tug, to ship the boat by rail or road, or to stay in the Mediterranean. One different possibility is to return through the Canal du Midi, and a description is given elsewhere, but a long sea passage will still remain, since that canal journey is westward rather than to the north.

The gaggle of oil storage tanks and chemical chimneys

customary to all large cities accompanies the first lock cut below Lyon. Then the Rhône whirls in, at speeds variously estimated at between four knots and twelve. The first figure is probably the more accurate, but the current is at times stiff enough to drag the channel marker buoys beneath the surface. Customarily all markers follow European maritime convention, with red marks on the starboard hand (on the right in canal parlance – always assuming that the helmsman is facing the bow), and black to be left to port by craft descending on the stream. It is useful to know this at the start of the first river section, where several rocks must be avoided, and left to port; and through Vienne, where the river is narrow.

There are occasional moorings against walls and quays. At Andance, an agreeable village, there is a small wharf below the church; then follow some attractive narrows, marked on the way by La Table du Roi, a rock partially awash upon which Louis IX, Crusader and founder of the Sorbonne, is said to have consumed his lunch while descending the river in 1248. Someone has since stuck a red and white pole on it, and this is left to starboard during the descent. Beyond the twin towns of Tournon and Tain l'Hermitage the valley widens, and the canalized sections that follow are unfortunately rather dull, being often dead straight and with high banks. But the locks are spectacular; the deepest of all, l'Ecluse Andre Blondel, or St-Pierre-de-Bollène, drops craft through 27m (89ft) with no more fuss than in one of the little locks back in the hinterland. Wandering around on the lockside one can sense through the soles of the feet the power being generated by the turbines; but it does not pay to linger too long, unless one is good at descending ladders.

There are castles at Roquemaure and Tour de l'Hers, while at Avignon, now bypassed by canal, there is the magnificent papal palace. Beaucaire follows, where the canal to Sète runs off to starboard; and then Romanesque Arles, which in addition to its architecture affords glimpses of the celebrated wildlife of the swamps. From Arles an old canal runs off to Port-de-Bouc near Marseilles, but final connection with that port was frustrated by the collapse of the Rove Tunnel in 1963. When built, in

The river at Avignon, recently bypassed by modernization work (*Nicholas Hopkinson*)

The Med

1927, this was the longest canal tunnel in the world, measuring 7120m. The width was 22m, but this proved too ambitious and restoration has yet to come.

Port St-Louis, a slightly anticlimatic place, affords the last stopping point before the Rhône joins the sea. It is held to be the customary site for re-stepping masts, but facilities for this purpose are few and the choice may lie between using a solitary tree or voyaging under engine to Marseilles. The canal from Port St-Louis should always be taken, however, rather than the uncertain river mouth.

Although this book is not primarily concerned with maritime pilotage, a word of caution may perhaps be uttered on the fierceness of Mediterranean winds, least this should go unsuspected. The land-locked Mediteranean creates a confused mass of air currents and pressures, and the weather situation is often locally unbalanced. Winds rise and fall quickly and at random, and can generate a confused and lumpy sea. Chief among the winds in southern France is the *mistral*, which blows from out of the Rhône valley itself, on average for one day in three. Although basically a northerly it tends to fan out in the delta. Most yachtsmen head for the balmier if crowded shores east of St-Tropez, which is sheltered from it; but attempts are now being made to lure people in the opposite direction, into new marinas built of crab-pink rock along the Languedoc coast. Recommended accessories are suntan oil, seasickness pills and plenty of money. Personally I prefer the older ports of Sète, Agde and Port Vendres.

Canal du Rhône à Sète
98km (61 miles) and 2 locks

A marshland waterway, running on the fringe of the Camargue, this route has undergone significant modernization, with the old entrance from Beaucaire bypassed by canalizing from Le Petit Rhone, a secondary channel of the main river. There are long straights and views of salt pans and buffalo. The thirteenth century town of Aigues-Mortes stands along the way, the first French seaport on the Mediterranean. Its doughty walls remain intact and may be easily walked around as there are convenient moorings close at hand. Like Rye and Winchelsea the town now finds itself brought inland by progressive silting, but there is access to the sea down the Chenal Maritime.

For the western part of its course the canal runs close inside the dunes, where after much endeavour, including the slaughter of many mosquitoes, the new coastal resorts of the Languedoc are now being developed. There are various streams connecting to the sea, but only one is officially navigable, other than at Aigues-Mortes. These channels run from the lakes on the inland side of the canal, sometimes creating a cross-current at the point of intersection. Near Sète the canal enters l'Etang de Thau, another and larger lake covered in the section devoted to the Canal du Midi.

The Brittany Waterways

A separate entity, the canal and river system of Brittany is worthy of a book of its own. It has survived by the skin of its teeth, traffic having gradually declined over the years. Recently, however, there has been a renewed interest, thanks largely to the Comité de Promotion Touristique des Canaux Bretons, which has encouraged not only seasonal pleasure cruising but a revival of the commercial traffic that prevents any waterway from becoming too whimsical.

A north-south route allows passage from the English Channel near St-Malo to the Bay of Biscay. Entry from the north is by way of the River Rance, now dammed off to provide electricity by means of tidal power. A lock provides access, and warning notices urge all afloat to keep well clear when the flow is towards the turbines. As elsewhere, masts must be lowered aboard sailing craft wishing to make the through passage. The canal itself is called the Canal d'Ille-et-Rance, and concludes in the River Vilaine.

The locks are smaller than on the Freycinet canals of central France. They measure 27.10m by 4.70m, and there are sixty-two in 246km (153 miles) between St-Malo and Tréhiguier on the north Brittany coast. There is a theoretical depth of 1.60m (5ft 3in), and a new barrage near the mouth of the Vilaine, also provided with a lock, will eliminate the groundings once customary at the southern end. To be on the safe side, however, anyone with a vessel drawing over 1.30m (4ft 3in) is advised to enquire as to the current state of play (see Appendix). The shallowest patches of all generally lie about 200m below each lock, where the silt settles from any water coming down.

This route is crossed by another waterway, from Nantes, near the mouth of the Loire. This runs northwest towards Brest, but alas does not reach it thanks to the construction of a dam across the route, the Barrage de Guerlédan.

Yacht on the River Rance, upstream of St-Malo.
As on all through routes the mast will have
to be lowered sooner or later – in this case
at the entrance to the Canal d'Ille-et-Rance,
where a low bridge restricts entry.

Despite its amputation, this navigation retains its old title of Canal de Nantes à Brest and there remains a further link with the sea again through the River Blavet, which connects with the seaport of Hennebont, near Lorient on the Biscay coast.

The two main routes, the north-south and the east-west, cross at the little market town of Redon. The Nantes à Brest locks are slightly smaller (26.50m by 4.70m east of Redon, 25.7m by 4.65m to the west), and there are many of them, 120 in all, although all save eighteen are between Redon and the barrage. Depth here is also reduced, with an estimated 1.35m (4ft 5in).

The River Loire may be explored officially as far as Bouchemaine, 85km above Nantes, but the venturesome may force a way upstream as far as Tours provided sufficient water can be found. The attractive rivers Mayenne and Sarthe, also neglected over the years, can be explored from Bouchemaine, by way of La Maine, as the waterway is at first called. There are forty-five locks in 134km (83 miles) up to the town of Mayenne, and twenty locks in 131km (81 miles) as far as Le Mans on the Sarthe.

Canal du Midi and Canal Latéral à la Garonne

Bordeaux to Sète, 504km (313 miles) and 154 locks

Although he died almost 300 years ago, Pierre-Paul Riquet remains a local hero in the Languedoc region of France. There are Riquet streets and Riquet monuments, Riquet plaques and Riquet cakeshops. There are Riquet cafés in which twentieth century artisans sit around like garden gnomes, marinating in the heat as their seventeenth century counterparts must have done.

Riquet was the Baron of Bonrepos, a tax collector who until he was fifty-five had done nothing likely to get himself remembered. When he died, almost inevitably penniless, at the age of seventy-six he had designed and built the coastal town of Sète, and had provided an overland water route between Atlantic and Mediterranean. He had directed 8000 labourers, and constructed numerous locks and staircases, having previously redirected a river and laid out 40 miles of water feeder from the north. Almost as an incidental he cut a 180 yard canal tunnel, probably the first ever, in the space of six days. His achievement in linking the two seas by 1681 preceded the entrée of James Brindley in England by 80 years.

Such is the Canal du Midi. At a later date, the temperamental River Garonne, which provided the westernmost half of the passage and which Riquet's canal entered at Toulouse, has itself been bypassed for the most part by another canal. Strictly speaking this is a separate waterway, the Latéral à la Garonne, but the two together, meeting at Toulouse, are often collectively known as the Midi, and there is little harm in that.

Entry from the western end is by the estuary of the Gironde, a sometimes dangerous place, but those who have successfully travelled so far by sea from England should have the necessary nautical knowhow, while the Admiralty Pilot for the region contains sufficient doom-laden advice to warn off the faint-hearted. At Ambes, within the mouth, the venturesome can turn off to explore the Dordogne, 120km up to St-Pierre d'Eyrand, but the more spectacular upper reaches are not accessible save to light craft.

On the Gironde there are mooring places at Royan, Port Bloc and Bordeaux itself, where the choice lies between locking into the docks, which are expensive and where I have been bitten repeatedly by mosquitoes, or at pontoons in the river, which from hereon becomes known as the Garonne.

Life can be rough on a pontoon, particularly as ships tend to pass in the night. The flood tide, when it arrives, is also preceded by a 2–3ft tidal wave. These difficulties notwithstanding, it is necessary to stop somewhere at Bordeaux if Customs have not been cleared elsewhere in France; and perhaps also to obtain a chart of the river as

Statue of Riquet at Toulouse (*Albert Barber*)

Docks at Bordeaux. The tide in the Garonne runs strongly.

Construction of the water-slope at Montech. The two locomotives push a plough or travelling gate up the slope. Special seals retain the water and a barge can remain floating before it. The device duplicates five conventional locks and is intended as a prototype for possible further water-slopes on new or enlarged canals. (*Andrew Darwin*)

there are pleasant moorings under overhanging trees. Similar spots may be found all along the Latéral which, although straight by comparison with the Midi east of Toulouse, is alluring enough in its own right. There are picturesque villages such as Meilhan and Mas d'Agenais, and towns such as Agen (a big aqueduct here) and Moissac, with its famous church. At Montech may be observed the world's first water-slope, whereby barges are lifted up the hillside by a giant bulldozer plough, drawing up water with a *péniche* inside, and propelled by diesel locomotives, one on each side of the slope. The water-slope is not considered suitable for 'yachts', which must work up the five old locks instead. All locks on the Latéral are now electrified, and in many cases automated, with striped barber's poles hanging from wires across the canal. These the boatman must seize in order to prepare the chamber. A green light indicates when a boat may enter and thereafter gates close and water enters by remote control. There are safety devices and if needs be human assistance, although this may have to be sought out. All the lock chambers on the route are notable for their eddying swirls, which demand a keen eye at the helm and a certain athleticism with the ropes.

From Montech an arm runs to the picturesque town of Montauban, but the remaining section into Toulouse is disappointingly dreary, while that city, though not without its splendours, provides high-speed motor racing for frustrated businessmen, and the passage by its ring road is a noisy one. One pair of staircase locks is actually in the centre of a dual carriageway, but there are wide basins for mooring, one of which, at the actual junction between Latéral and Midi, formerly gave access to the Garonne.

Dimensionally, the Midi is a sub-standard waterway (see Appendix), unlike the Latéral where the bulk of the traffic plies, and which has recently been modernized and electrified in the manner described. The Midi itself – Riquet's Midi – is following. This could be a pity, for the old works do not take easily to the concrete that is added to lengthen the locks. The process is being slowed, however, and is to be completed in stages over many years. The old atmosphere may thus survive a little longer.

far as Castets, 54km (34 miles) upstream, where the canal is entered.

Otherwise the popular advice is to follow a *péniche*, but however slow their progress in the canal, they tend to roar up the river and can be difficult to pursue. The less speedy should proceed as cautiously as a five knot flood tide allows, following signs and not cutting any corners, and aiming to arrive before high water at Castets.

The first lock at Castets-en-Dorthe offers tranquility and the three in close succession form a lovely flight, and

Midi locks have elliptical sides and are often arranged as staircases (*Albert Barber*)

From Toulouse eastward the locks are elliptical, with curving sides, so built as to resist the earth pressure in much the same way that an arched bridge or dam offers greater strength than a straight one. As elsewhere, the lock-keepers work one side, boat crews the other. Frequently the keeper is a lady, and usually there is a dog, sometimes several, although Midi dogs are not malevolent, and are more inclined to snooze than to bite. There are also fowl, yattering hens or flat-footed geese, while near at hand a local housewife will be scrubbing the family laundry at one of the low stone platforms so thoughtfully provided at the waterside. It is absolutely *de rigeur* to slow down and make no wash while passing these.

One of the most thankless jobs in southern France must be that of paint salesman. Paint is applied to timber in the same way that an English canteen serves up rice, that is to say sparingly and as a very great favour. On the Midi buildings the prevalent colour is a thinly-spread green, pasted over the shutters and doors and peeled and mellowed to an almost subliminal olive. A cast iron plaque over each doorway lists the distances in each direction.

A mooring at night near one of these locks provides a full range of effects: starlight overhead, rushing water over the gates, the rattle of a tribe of cicadas and the snores of some indeterminate beast locked in a shed. For much of the route the towpath is shaded by large plane trees, packed tight in line, and originally planted to protect donkeys and mules from the glare of the sun. The effect is rich, and nowhere more so than at the beautiful Ecluse de l'Ocean, the last lock before the summit. A mile away a Riquet monument, a stone needle bearing plaques, marks the original inspiration. Nearby the feeder canals may be seen. The supply of water was Riquet's obsession, and thanks to this the canal never runs dry despite the extensive use of staircases, which are generally much more wasteful than separated locks.

Although electrification has been provided in some cases, as at the four-chamber staircase at Castlenaudary, and the seven-lock descent near Beziers, elsewhere the hand-wound *vannes* are exceedingly stiff, and the crew intent upon a fast passage will need to be in strict training.

The trees lining the canal were originally planted as shade for the mules and towing horses.

Castelnaudary
(*Albert Barber*)

In view of the labour involved it is important to signify any intention of stopping, for each keeper telephones ahead to prepare the way, and the next one in line may toil away needlessly, and keep some other vessel waiting into the bargain.

Castelnaudary has an enormous basin one mile around the perimeter. There are trees on one side and the churches and houses of the town on the other, all piled in an impressive heap. The place is noted for its *cassoulet*, a grossly over-rated dish comprised almost totally of dull white beans and sold with a defensive vehemence at almost every restaurant in the place.

Carcassonne, twenty-five miles down the line, is another medieval walled city, partially reconstructed and deservedly sought out by the tourist for its profusion of turrets, battlements and draw-bridges. There are trips around the ramparts, with minimal safety precautions but good views for those with a head for heights. Originally the canal avoided Carcassonne, owing to a dispute with the local authorities, but in the early nineteenth century amends were made and the waterway re-routed using the forced labour of Prussian prisoners of war. Barges are often to be seen loading wine in the basin before the town.

Yet another rural section follows, and in it is a long winding stretch of over thirty miles without locks. This the barges attempt to reach before nightfall so that they may soldier on out of hours. I have lain in a hire cruiser at Capestang, a humble wine-producing village along the way, and watched a barge come through the bridge at one o'clock in the morning, with a dramatic shaft of light through the arch and a brief glimpse of a spidery figure whirling the wheel as it passed. Thus it pays to moor well clear of the main channel and never, as anywhere where heavy craft are at large, on the outside of a bend.

From this section a branch canal leads down through Narbonne, once on the coast itself, to join the sea at the unattractive port of La Nouvelle. It provides a short cut to salt water, with thirteen locks in 32km (20 miles), but there are several obstacles on the way, including a crossing of the swift-flowing River Aude, some narrows and a

Grape-pickers by the canalside near Capestang

Midi tradition is brusquer than on the canals of central France. Intermediate gates are left open and a veritable millrace allowed to rush straight through one chamber and into the next. This can be awe-inspiring to those coming uphill.

A completely circular lock near Agde allows barges to rotate and leave through a different pair of gates in order to descend a short branch to this ancient fishing port. In this coastal region the canal undergoes a change in character, the land becoming swampy and almost Abyssinian, on a par with the canals of the Camargue not very far away. Dragonflies drone past and the odd snake suns itself upon the surface. The Pyrennean foothills have dropped away from the horizon; the trees are suddenly absent and the canal stretches towards the sky. A final straight leads out into the nine mile lake, the shimmering Étang de Thau.

The lake is shallow, but not sufficiently so to bother any craft capable of navigating the canal. It has, however, many poles for oysters, and buoys and nets, while the *mistral*, when blowing, can create a short and nasty sea. My own experiences, however, have always coincided with windless calms. A number of small ports line the lake's northern edge, and of these Mèze is perhaps the most attractive, less advanced in its sophistication than other Mediterranean pleasure ports and with a large basin in which mussels may be found.

Sète stands on a conical hill at the eastern end of the lake. This is a town which still, thank goodness, faces the port and the canals cut through the isthmus. It is entered from the lake by passing beneath two large lift bridges which allow a clearance of two metres or so, depending upon the level of the lake. Opening of these bridges takes place at nine in the morning and five at night, neatly coinciding with the rush hour in both instances, so that trucks and buses pile up in the roadways around the town.

Inside are several canals, packed with craft and in which it can be difficult to find a mooring. The determined may wish to pass on through the town to the fishing port and outer harbour, where an incredible din takes place as fishing boats shove their way towards the market. Every-

tricky bridge at Narbonne.

For vessels continuing along the main line there is the short tunnel of Malpas, which Riquet's men hacked out more or less when no one was looking, in order to confound the cynics who said that it could not be done. At Beziers, once again castellated, and where all 60,000 inhabitants were massacred by the army of Simon de Montfort, there is the seven lock staircase of Fonserannes, which faces the battlements from across the valley. Once the canal descended all the way to the River Orb, but now an aqueduct built by Vauban leads craft across the river from the bottom of the flight. Vessels cannot pass each other within the staircase and so may have to wait, but the

Market stall at Sète (*Albert Barber*)

Seven lock staircase of Fonserannes, Béziers (*Albert Barber*)

one in Sète appears to shout, and to do things with panache, be it the wielding of a hose or steering the little motorized fishing dories which progress to and fro on pointless journeys in the town canals. The Sètois themselves speak French with a Lancashire accent, or at any rate with a harder emphasis on the vowels. They are also good cooks, and a number of the restaurants that line the banks can be recommended. The strange feature of this exuberant centre, where water-borne jousting is performed upon the most elaborate vessels during feast days, and where every action and word is *fortissimo*, is that the fish that they catch are all tiny.

Thus the traveller from the Atlantic can end his inland journey at a true canal town, the French equivalent of Stourport, although in far better condition. There are sunny houses crammed along the waterside, amazonian ladies with bronze hairdos pushing the fish barrows, and for those tempted to take a swim, jelly-fish the size of chamber pots. Sète provides a zestful finale to a voyage through the Canal Entre Deux Mers.

Sète. Fishing boats crowd the wharves.

Mèze on the Étang de Thau, the long salt lake within the sand dunes near Sète

The Moselle near Trier

Finale: the Moselle

French portion, 106km (66 miles) and 10 locks

Arthur left France to the North, shuffling into a little lock near Nancy that gave access to the River Moselle. We had spent over six months under way on the French canals, which by being a working system provide a harmony of leisure and purpose that is difficult to find in other walks. Our crews had ranged from grandmothers to babes in arms, from tax officers to practitioners of yoga; fifty-five people had come in all, some more than once. From experience I now know that if the crew ever exceeds eight it is impossible to step ashore, order a meal or sit down for an uninterrupted thirty seconds without having nervous attacks. I sold a half-share in the boat back to Mike, and with it more than half the responsibility since each thought the other was doing the worrying.

The Moselle, which starts in scrubland and ironworks, quickly develops into a glorious waterway. By this time Roger Pilkington's excellent *Waterways in Europe* had been procured. It led us through a series of pools and backwaters to a gracious mooring in the city of Metz, and it also itemized the many superb reaches in the Luxembourg and German territory beyond. The French portion of the river has been navigable for some time, bringing coal and ore to the great steelworks of Hagondange and Thionville, where throughout the night there are thunderous crashes as of tank battalions being dropped from a very great height. But beyond this point the Moselle is a new and international waterway opened only in 1964, and bearing an enormous traffic without damaging the environment one jot.

This river and the Rhine beyond demostrate the differences in administrative temperament. These are epitomized by procedures at Apach Lock, the border point. The

German locomotive at Bullay

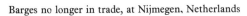

Barges no longer in trade, at Nijmegen, Netherlands

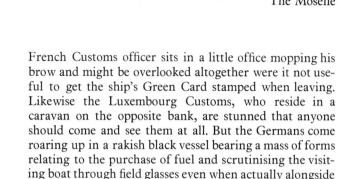

French Customs officer sits in a little office mopping his brow and might be overlooked altogether were it not useful to get the ship's Green Card stamped when leaving. Likewise the Luxembourg Customs, who reside in a caravan on the opposite bank, are stunned that anyone should come and see them at all. But the Germans come roaring up in a rakish black vessel bearing a mass of forms relating to the purchase of fuel and scrutinising the visiting boat through field glasses even when actually alongside it.

There are further differences from here on. Whereas in France all was free, at the locks of Luxembourg and Germany we paid ten marks each time unless sharing with commercial craft. On the railway alongside there were steam locomotives still, the Germans not being so foolish as to scrap machinery still in good working order. But the miles of vineyard, the film set housing of Bernkastel and the slopes of Trittenheim all provide a splendid background.

Later, as *Arthur* whirled down the Rhine and into Dordrecht in Holland, a water crossroads where thousands of tons float by every minute, we were to appreciate the enormous force and vigour of the Continental waterway system. Where could we go to next? Back through Belgium; or into Germany again, across the *meers* of Friesland? Or perhaps when the new canal is opened from the River Main, through this and into the Danube? There is so much left to see.

Fully navigable for less than ten years, the Moselle carries a healthy traffic. *Arthur* is the boat at the back of the lock.

Appendix

Suitable Craft for Canals

Choosing a boat is the traditional how-long-is-a-piece-of-string topic in yachting books. As indicated earlier the requirements of the French canals are not always compatible with the seagoing entailed in reaching them. A rugged iron or steel barge is well adapted, but those with a salt water capacity take a little seeking out in Britain. Other possibilities are to cross the Channel in a seaworthy vessel and to accept her shortcomings, if any, on the canals; or to take a smaller boat to the Continent by ferry on a trailer. Alternatively, craft can now be hired on a number of inland waterways in France. But first of all it may be useful to consider some broad general points.

HULL MATERIALS   Timber, although an excellent material, is rarely found in new craft nowadays because of the labour and expense of construction. Old wooden working boats are liable to rot and nailsickness, and must always be approached with caution. Of all craft, those built of wood should always be acquired 'subject to survey', with an independent surveyor reporting to the purchaser before the deal is settled. Timber is generally a more expensive material to maintain, and plywood in particular must be well cared for. But there are a number of suitable old wooden craft around, and in the smaller sizes a sound clinker-built lifeboat conversion, for instance, fulfills many of the requirements for inland cruising.

Fibreglass, although durable under certain conditions, is vulnerable to abrasion. Craft should be protected with a thick all-round rubbing rail at the gunwales with, if possible, further protection at water level. One advantage of fibreglass, or glass-reinforced plastic to use a more accurate term, is that it permits the construction of relatively light craft suitable for trailing. However, 'glass' boats require careful fitting out: cleats and rails need to be firmly attached, not with screws but by bolts passing through wooden or metal reinforcement pads under the decks or superstructure. This is most important.

Ferrocement has become recognized as a practical material in hull construction, and can be used to produce hull forms as sophisticated as any, and at a relatively low cost. Tempting though it may be (and some fine ferro motor and sailing vessels have been built), it can abrade and flake in the locks, unless well fendered.

Iron or steel are the most suitable materials of all, being resistant to rubbing, collision with lock walls, etc. Such, at any rate, is the conclusion of barge operators all over the Continent, for no other material may be seen, save in very old craft which are occasionally of wood. If buying second hand, look for corrosion and worn plates, particularly under the stern on the 'right-hand side'.

HULL FORM AND STEERING POSITION   With a draft preferably of no more than 4ft, straight sides and an upright bow a boat should be able to go almost anywhere on the inland system, and the absence of flare or overhang will save damage through being caught up on lock walls. In contemplating wear and tear it is useful to recall that when a lock is full of water the stone coping alongside is often just a few inches high. Small craft swinging round may overhang this wall and rub or scrape. Similarly, projecting sterngear can also get caught. Ideally both rudder and propeller should be tucked beneath the hull, and in such a position that they can also survive a grounding. In this respect single engine installations are preferable to twin screws, which require cautious handling particularly when coming alongside or passing near a sloping bank.

It has been found over the years that a steering position near the stern allows the most precise handling, if only because the entire vessel is under the steerer's eye and any swing or turn may be more easily gauged. For small craft a tiller is more efficient, in that it transmits the feel of the ship and permits a quick and positive response. Its disadvantage is that it does not allow sitting in comfort, as in a wheelhouse. It is also most convenient, and some would say essential, that the steerer can see the lockside and have all activities under his eye when inside a lock chamber. Superstructures ideally should be uncluttered, and although safety rails are a blessing at sea or where children are around, they tend to impede the hurling and making fast of ropes, or access to lockside ladders. Strong cleats or bollards are required, with as much clear space around them as possible.

SIZE AND SPEED   The majority of locks will pass a vessel measuring 38.5m by 5.05m (126ft by 16ft 6in) and in theory any craft of this size can navigate between the Channel and the Mediterranean – provided that draft and overhead clearances are within acceptable limits. However certain waterways are sub-standard and the locks are smaller, most notably on the Canal du Midi, the centre section of the Nivernais, and the waterways of Brittany. Maximum acceptable dimensions are as follows:

Canal du Nivernais: length 30m (98ft 5in), beam 5.05m (16ft 6in), draft 1.2m (3ft 11in), height above waterline 2.7m (8ft 8in).

Canal du Midi: length 30m (98ft 5in), beam 5.25m (17ft 1in), draft 1.6m (5ft 3in), height above waterline 3.4m at centre and 2.0m at sides (11ft 2in and 7ft 6in).
Brittany canals: length 26m (85ft 3in), beam 4.5m (14ft 9in), draft 1.3m (4ft 3in), height above waterline 2.3m at centre and 2.0m at sides (8ft 2in and 7ft 6in).

Other waterways: length 38.5m (126ft), beam 5.05m (16ft 6in), draft 1.8m (5ft 11in), height above waterline 3.4m (11ft 2in) except Canal du Bourgogne which is 3.0m at centre and 2.2m at sides (9ft 10in and 7ft 2in).

This is perhaps a suitable point at which to emphasize the obvious: that the bigger the vessel, the more she will cost to run. Ropes must be thicker, paint has to be applied in greater quantities, insurance premiums are higher, and so on. Thus, in many senses, the smaller the boat the better. But it is a great mistake to have a vessel incapable of carrying people in reasonable comfort, dignity and privacy. Once again the prospective captain should visualize a series of wet days in dreary surroundings, and contemplate their effects upon the boat that he has in mind.

A vessel capable of maintaining seven or eight knots will be able to keep pace with the bulk of the traffic between locks on the bigger rivers of the North, although craft of lesser speeds will merely suffer the odd delay as traffic locks through ahead. On the canals speeds are much lower, with an official limit of just over three knots (see Boat Handling).

If the Rhône is to be ascended without a tow, a speed through the water of seven or eight knots is necessary, but such speeds are not required elsewhere. *Arthur* had a maximum of six knots and that, by and large, has proved quite sufficient for the rest of the network.

TYPES OF ENGINE   It is now widely recognized that a diesel inboard engine is the most reliable and economical form of unit. It should be installed with the utmost care, on firm and substantial bearers, paying close attention to the manufacturer's instructions and with the shaft accurately in line. A petrol engine is initially slightly cheaper, and less given to noise and vibration than a diesel. But the fuel is more expensive, and the risk of fire and explosion is greater.

Outboard engines, although compact, have a higher fuel consumption again; while the outdrive, or inboard/outboard, which combines an inboard engine with propulsion through the transom, is in the same way dependent upon the application of power for control. Being rudderless, craft with outboards or outdrives can be awkward to handle at very low speeds, while the protruding propulsion leg is also vulnerable.

SEAWORTHINESS   A seagoing boat should be capable of facing rough weather. She must be stable and able to move forward when the wind blows, as opposed to backwards or sideways. Good characteristics in seagoing motor craft are controllability, strength to withstand pounding, and a powerful engine, well installed.

But these are enormous generalizations. Seagoing is a wide topic, to which countless books have been devoted, and it can only be treated here by stating, perhaps pompously, that it is important to have someone aboard with experience of the sea and appreciation of what is entailed. That said, it must be admitted that *Arthur*'s own coastal voyage was by no means the epitome of salty wisdom and virtue; the boat needed greater power, and a more secure steering position. However the chapter on that journey does perhaps indicate some of the factors involved. Careful preparation, the lashing down of all movables, a knowledge of the engine and in particular of the fuel filtration system are all prerequisites. Understanding and practice in the basic principles of navigation are also essential.

There are various yacht delivery firms that will undertake such a passage; these advertise in boating magazines and will give quotations. It is perhaps invidious to recommend particular companies; some are good and some are awful. Those with a record of successful and business-like operation are the ones to contact.

SAILING CRAFT   Sailing vessels are perhaps the best adapted for a sea crossing, but require some modification for canals. The mast must be lowered or lifted out by crane upon arrival, and the rigging, spars and sails may then be something of an encumbrance. However many sailing craft are well enough adapted to inland waterways, the prime requirements being easy handling under power, sufficiently low draft, and plenty of fend-offs.

FINDING A SECOND-HAND BARGE   Rugged iron or steel barges are occasionally to be found in Britain, although ironically many of these are Dutch in origin. A 62-footer advertised at £3500 in 1973 was fitted out for the storage of live eels, but had good forward accommodation for the crew, a wheelhouse and a powerful modern engine. Other Dutch craft in the UK, this time with the holds converted for living aboard, measured 85ft by 16ft and 100ft by 17ft 6in, and asking prices were respectively £8000 and £17,000. With inflation figures had doubled by 1980.

At the other end of the scale a 70ft English barge on the Humber, rough but apparently sound and with an engine installed, was sold unconverted for £2500, while vessels like *Arthur* may occasionally be seen advertised at similar prices in boating magazines. It should be added that craft of the narrow boat type of the English canals are not at all suitable either for the sea crossing or for several Continental rivers, being insufficiently stable for choppy water.

The working boats of the French canals are generally too large for pleasure use, but smaller barges may still be found in the Netherlands. Conducting such operations at a distance can be a long-winded business and the most satisfactory procedure is to look around personally at an inland port (practically every town is an inland port in Holland), and having made basic contact, to put the transaction into the hands of a Dutch solicitor.

A typical vessel *De Goede* (*Good Hope*), which *Arthur* moored alongside in Nijmegen and which it transpired was up for sale, measured 22.5m by 5m (74ft by 16ft 5in) with a draft of 1m (3ft 3in) unladen. She had a steel hull, built in 1903 but in very good condition, with agreeable accommodation fore and aft, a big wheelhouse, and with hatch covers over the hold, which was unconverted; the single cylinder engine was fitted with blowlamp starting. Her young and patently honest owner had been using the vessel in trade and hoped to buy something larger. He was asking 22,000 guilders, about £5,000 today (1980).

TRAILING   If taking a boat by trailer, the matter should be confirmed with the owner's insurance company, and the certificate amended if necessary. The Channel ferry bookings must be made in good time and a Carnet obtained (see 'Formalities' and 'Addresses').

Launching sites are an uncertain quantity. There are several on the rivers, but few on canals unless the boat can be launched over a low quay. The French Government Tourist Office publishes a useful leaflet with a map showing the locations of clubs, and wherever motorboating or water-skiing are indicated there is usually a suitable slope close at hand.

HIRE COMPANIES   Hiring is probably the most convenient form of boating for those not able to mount a major expedition. People tend to gasp at the prices asked, the operators responding with rueful expressions on the shortness of the season, appalling overheads, crippling taxation, and so on. Charges exceed those in Britain by a considerable margin, a measure of the shifts in exchange rates in recent years.

HOTEL BARGES, or *hotel-pêniches*, offer all the facilities of a hotel (or in the case of the smaller craft, a country cottage) with cabin accommodation and all meals provided. In many cases a coach or mini-bus runs in conjunction with the barge, for excursions. Such operations are now numerous, the larger craft tending to run on wide rivers, the smaller on the more intimate canals.

Addresses for both self-drive and hotel-barge operators may be obtained from the French Government Tourist Office, 178 Piccadilly, London W1.

Boat Handling Inland

Everybody makes mistakes in handling a boat. Just as an ace cricketer can score a duck, so does the 'expert' helmsman nudge a bridge or lock, or miscalculate the drift on wind or current.

A golden rule is to throttle back early. Good control can often be obtained by losing speed and then edging the boat forward again. At the same time there will be a greater opportunity to gauge conditions. In a river, safe handling is always better achieved by turning into the current – with a look over the shoulder first to check that no one is about to overtake. If coming alongside a quay a cautious approach is naturally preferred, in case of shallows.

Meeting another vessel in a narrow canal is a common enough experience. As always it pays to slow right down. The rule of the road is to keep to the right, or in nautical parlance to leave the other craft to port. If the other vessel is a laden *pêniche* she will need much more of the channel, but it is wise to pass fairly close in order to avoid grounding. The *pêniche* helmsman will probably gun his engine as the other vessel passes his stern and this will draw the 'yacht' back into the centre of the channel. Naturally, if a wider spot can be seen it pays to linger in this and to pass the *pêniche* there. The gesture will be appreciated.

Very occasionally a heavy and unwieldly vessel may find it convenient to pass on the 'wrong' side, either because of a sharp bend, or if in a fast-flowing river, in order to dodge the current when pressing upstream. On rivers the appropriate signal is a blue flag or board displayed on the starboard (right) side, the side you are expected to pass. If doubt arises, two blasts on the siren signify an intention (on the part of the vessel making the signal) to turn to port, that is to 'keep to the left'.

Overtaking a laden vessel is sometimes a delicate matter, for it is absolutely *infra dig* to do so if the process will unduly delay the *pêniche* at the next lock. It is courteous also to advise the lock-keeper of the situation so that the chamber may be made ready for the vessel overtaken.

The most acceptable method of overtaking is to hover a reasonable distance astern until beckoned past. The *péniche* will then probably ease off for a few moments while the 'yacht' overtakes as quickly as she can. It is possible for two craft to be sucked together, so it is wise not to pass *too* close, and to be vigilant on the helm.

Speed limits are often loosely interpreted, not least by empty commercial craft which tend to blast along as fast as they are able. The officially sanctioned limits are 6km/hr (3¼mph) on canals and 10km/hr (6mph) on rivers, with greater speeds allowed on the Seine and Rhône.

The real criterion is a vessel's wash. A breaking wave undermines the banks and causes insidious damage. Any wash can disturb craft at a mooring, unsettle anglers or drench the washerwomen who use municipal facilities by the canalside. Wash is sometimes unavoidable, but every canal user will experience someone's thoughtlessness on this matter sooner or later, and will know how enraging this is.

Locks bear heavily in people's minds, but are not normally difficult. Stout lines are needed, and should always be made fast in such a way that they can be released when under load. A good method is to have lines with a large loop spliced in one end, and this may be placed on a bollard on shore. The other end may be made fast with figure-of-eight turns around a stout cleat or bollards, taking care that these cannot jam. Ropework is the key to inland boat handling. Few knots are needed – a bowline and the figure-of-eight will suffice for most situations – but it pays to be systematic in coiling and throwing.

On hand-operated locks the keeper will supervise, but boat crews are expected to lend a hand. It is not the keeper's responsibility to take or tend any lines.

Tunnels vary in administration. Some have towing to a strict timetable, some whenever traffic merits, and occasionally a pleasure boat may be allowed to proceed under her own power. Short tunnels are usually unsupervised. In lieu of a tough hull, plenty of fendering should be used, while a wide-beam headlight will pick out the section of the arch when craft are passing through on their own.

In towing, each crew must provide its own line to the vessel in front, and once again it is important to attach the near end in such a manner that it can be released while still in tension.

Mooring is best accomplished to bollards on shore. Where these are not properly spaced, or where only one may be found, it is sometimes acceptable to put both bow and stern lines to the same one. Other craft will suck the vessel out in passing, so good fenders will be needed. Obviously separate bow and stern lines are preferable, with springs if possible – duplicate ropes from each mooring point on shore to the further cleats on the boat, in order to act as braces against any surge forwards or back.

Trees, posts and fences also offer themselves, with the obvious proviso that there should be no damage to property or obstruction of the towpath. It is quite amazing how many anglers wish to pass once lines have been put across their track.

If using a bollard also in use by another vessel, it is the custom for each newcomer to pass the noose of his line up through the other before laying it over the bollard. In that way either vessel can cast off without disturbing the other's lines.

Security at a mooring is a worry to many Britons, conditioned alas to hooliganism and pilfering. The problem is far less acute in France, save perhaps in the largest cities. If in doubt it is wise to lock up, but clearing the decks and fiddling with catches is often tedious, and on *Arthur* we rarely bothered. If *pêniches* are near at hand the risks are even less, while the safest mooring of all is actually alongside one. It is wise to ask first, as *pêniches* have a habit of leaving at a quarter to six the following morning.

Services

Diesel fuel is sold at waterside points on canals and rivers where barges operate, generally at major centres or at junctions such as Berry-au-Bac or St-Jean-de-Losne.

They have metered pumps and long hoses with a pistol type nozzle, but, alas, this *Mazout* or *Gasoil Domestique* is no longer available to yachts and fully-taxed fuel has to be sought, like petrol, at relatively inconvenient garages in the towns. At certain ports and stations fuel may be bought on a Shell Letter of Credit, available from Shell International Petroleum Co., SP/3113, Shell Centre, London SE1.

Bottled gas is likewise distributed at the waterside, sometimes at a lock-keeper's cottage which will display a manufacturer's plate. There are an infinity of different brands, but *Butagaz* is among the most common, and has the advantage of having the same threads and fittings as British Calor gas.

Drinking water is widely available, and most lock cottages have a supply somewhere, if pressed. The occasional one provides a hose.

French garages are enormously resourceful. Welding, grinding, forging and drilling are often undertaken by the same man. *Arthur* had a thermostat housing, cracked through over-tightening, welded in a quarter of an hour – a tricky job with a crystalline casting. At 5.45 on a Friday evening, the Garage Peugeot at Cercy-la-Tour set to and fabricated two engine mounting lugs at a charge of 8 francs. Such services can be commended.

Shoreside rubbish and toilet facilities are noticeable for their absence; and dustbins, when provided at all, are rarely emptied. Under the circumstances the decent thing to do is to bury all ordures. Chemical toilets are arguably the most civilized to carry on board, although the chemical used is sometimes destructive in itself, to water life. Commercial craft just pump out into the canal, and nobody thinks anything of it – save British visitors – since it has all been going on for years.

Deck Equipment

Over and above the items normally carried on boats, the following may be useful for canal travel.

Ropes   *Arthur* had 60ft bow and stern lines, each with a noose at one end. In addition a 60ft light line for throwing and a heavy 100ft spare line are also carried. All are of artificial fibre of a non-stretching variety that is easy to coil and knot, and is fairly kindly to the hands. Though smaller craft may use lighter ropes (*Arthur*'s are of 3in circumference) they need to be of considerable length for use in locks, and 50–60ft is necessary for bow and stern lines, even on small vessels.

Shafts, boathooks and planks   Without some means of poling off, the occasional grounding, which is usually in a river, can take on the status of a marooning. *Arthur's* long shaft is an 18-footer from the English waterways, but many pleasure craft would have nowhere to keep such a thing. The longer the better all the same. A boathook should never be used against other craft, least of all its sharp end.

A gangplank is handy at sloping quaysides and banks.

Fenders   Many plastic yacht fenders are far too small, and thick used motor tyres are often better, and very cheap or free. They may be bored for hanging ropes with a brace and bit, with further holes at the bottom to drain away any water. Two big tyres threaded together one above the other provide an even more satisfactory fend-off. The hanging lines should be really tough. Tyres tend to mark the boat's side, but not so badly or permanently as rough stones or nails projecting from a quay, and plastic fend-offs tend to get brushed aside by such obstructions.

Flags   As explained, bright flags at the bow announce a vessel among the shrubbery of a bend. In addition, every visiting craft should fly her national ensign at the stern. For the majority of Britons this will be the Red Ensign. As a courtesy, the National Flag of France is also flown from some miniature yardarm or equivalent position, on the starboard side.

A blue flag, about a metre square, is necessary on certain rivers when passing on the 'wrong' side. It is customarily flown on a pole projecting horizontally on the starboard side when the situation demands.

A large red flag conveys the sobering news that a vessel has broken down or has some other special reason for asking other vessels to slow when passing. Pessimists may care to carry one.

A yellow flag requests Customs clearance when entering the country.

Dinghy   For ferrying ropes across shallows, for better access to the propeller, for rescuing people, and for swimming from, a small dinghy is invaluable. The tiny moulded *Sportyak I* carried aboard *Arthur*, though not by any standards a seaworthy vessel, is excellent for inland waters, being unsinkable, even when filled with water, and light enough to be heaved on board. Towing a dinghy is the road to disaster, not least in locks, and such a boat should always be carried on deck.

Hooters   A horn is a great asset, for awakening slumbering lock staff and for apprising craft at the other end of winding one-way sections. But it needs to be powerful.

Spotlight   Night navigation is often forbidden and generally ill-advised, although it is easy to get caught out and a powerful lamp can pick out a mooring in the dusk. It is also useful in fog, and if mounted high can demonstrate one's presence within a lock, or illuminate tunnel roofs and arches. A further wide-angle beam is useful in tunnels.

Miscellaneous   Water hoses must be long – say, 60 ft – and with a Continental fitting. An energetic alternative is a five-gallon plastic jerry-can for carrying to and fro, and as an emergency supply.

Spades, a heavy hammer, spikes and crowbars have all come in handy on *Arthur*, for dealing with protrusions on quaysides, lavatorial excavation, and so on. Binoculars are extremely useful in making out lock signals, particularly where a choice between two chambers must be made from a long way upstream. A powerful magnet offers some hope of retrieving lock handles and other valuables from the bottom.

A good bike saves hours, particularly on the long searches for bread that characterize voyages through remote country areas. Two bicycles offer the prospect of exploring in company. Wide, heavy duty tyres are better for knobbly towpaths; baskets, panniers and elastic cord allow goods to be carried. Hub-type gears are unusual

in France, and finding spares can be awkward.

Waterproof wallets enable maps and reference books to be kept or used on deck.

Safety Equipment

People wax very earnest on safety, with some reason. Explosion, fire, sinking and drowning are, alas, always a possibility, though statistically less so than accidents on the road – or in the home. The following items can be recommended for inland craft.

Buckets for baling far more effectively than any electric, or motor-driven pump, which will block up with sludge or wood shavings just when it is needed most.

Fire extinguishers   Big ones are infinitely preferable to little ones. Many pleasure craft carry little aerosol extinguishers that could scarcely deal with a burning fat-pan. There is no such thing as a small fire; it is merely a big fire getting started. Ten, or better still, twenty pound extinguishers offer a fighting chance. There are many different types, and until recently those containing dry powder have been held to be the most effective. But BCF, a gas which is stored as a liquid, is now being recognized as being more likely to permeate beneath floorboards or an engine. Powder emerges as a jet and does not filter behind solid objects. It also blows back into the face of the operator.

Automatic detection and extinguishing systems are sometimes fitted to small craft. Their operation must be truly automatic, and should not depend upon the throwing of switches, turning on devices in the engine compartment, and so on.

Gas and engine installations   Bottled gas, being denser than air, can escape into bilges and remain there as an explosion hazard. It must therefore be carried outside, or if within the boat in a container venting over the side through a large aperture. Any flexible gas piping must be of an approved type, as available at authorized dealers in

Britain, but copper piping, free of joints, should really be used throughout. Engine fitments must be fire resistant. Filter containers ought not to be of plastic or glass, while vent pipes from fuel tanks should be led outside, and preferably covered with flame-proof gauze.

Life-rings   Two are kept aboard *Arthur* for throwing to anyone in the water. These not only provide support, but help to mark the spot during the pandemonium of turning the boat around in a river. The horseshoe shaped type are easier to climb into.

Engine stop control   Anyone in the water runs the risk of being struck by the propeller. Unless the engine can be put positively out of gear an engine stop control is necessary, and lest the skipper should himself be in the water it is advisable that all the crew be acquainted with these risks and arrangements.

Torch, knife and first aid kit are fairly obvious items; but a bread knife is often the most efficient means of severing a rope, while first aid kits should be checked for the presence of ointments, antiseptics and plasters in addition to the bandages that are all some proprietary boxes contain.

Addresses

The French Government Tourist Office, 178 Picadilly, London W1, provides good leaflets with maps, and will answer general queries.

The Touring Club de France, which may be joined at the same address, or at 65 Avenue de la Grande-Armée, Paris 16, will privide further assistance. The TCF maintains a motorboating section and has a number of bases in France.

Les Canaux Bretons, Chambre de Commerce de Rennes, Place Honoré-Commeureuc, 35000 Rennes may be additionally contacted regarding the waterways of Britanny.

Le Ministere de l'Equipement, Direction des Ports Maritimes et des Voies Navigables, 2e bureau, boulevard Saint-Germain, Paris 7 will answer queries regarding the administration of the waterways.

Le Bureau des Douanes pour le Tourisme, 182 rue Saint-Honoré, Paris 1 may be contacted regarding Customs enquiries.

The Royal Yachting Association, Victoria Way, Woking, Surrey protects British boating interests, and will advise on ownership/registration (see Formalities).

The Automobile Association, Fanum House, Leicester Square, London WC2 can provide documentation regarding trailing.

Books, Maps and Guides

The *Guide de la Navigation Interieure*, published by Librairie Berger-Levrault, 5 rue Auguste-Comte, Paris 6, in two volumes, but now out of print, should be snapped up if found. Excellent strip maps with notes, for individual waterways, may be bought in France at town bookshops, chandlers and boatyards; and in the U.K. from chart agents such as J. D. Potter Ltd, 145 Minories, London EC3 or Stanford's, 12 Long Acre, London WC2E 9LP.

Cruising French Waterways by Hugh McKnight, to be published by Stanford Maritime in early 1984, is a detailed guide to the canals and rivers and their environs: main Belgian waterways are also included.

Waterways in Europe by Roger Pilkington, published by John Murray, covers many French waterways, with details of mooring sites etc, and has similar, highly expert notes on Belgium, Germany, Sweden and a portion of Holland. It would be churlish not to acknowledge the influence of this book, or the many in Dr Pilkington's *Small Boat* series (*Small Boat through France, in Southern France, to Luxembourg*, etc) which fill in the historical and background details, and which provided the inspiration for *Arthur's* voyages.

General guides to France are widely available, the most notable being published by the Michelin company, and some of these are now translated into English. The detailed maps also published by Michelin, and widely available on the Continent, will enable the traveller to seek out individual villages and note the lie of the land.

For the sea crossing the navigator will require *Reed's Nautical Almanac* and detailed charts. Of the relevant yachtsmen's pilot books, *Brittany and Channel Islands Cruising Guide* (Stanford Maritime) also includes the Brittany canals. The coast east of Cherbourg is covered by *Normandy Harbours and Pilotage: Calais to Cherbourg* and *North Sea Harbours and Pilotage: Calais to Den Helder*, published by Adlard Coles Ltd. The useful *Cruising Association Handbook* and *Notes on French Inland Waterways* are obtainable from booksellers or the Cruising Association, Ivory House, St Katherine Dock, London E1 9AT.

Pilot books, almanacs, canal and Michelin maps and guides, and travel and guide books for France are available from Stanford's Map Shop, 12 Long Acre, London WC2E 9LP (836-7863).

Formalities

Arrival in France by sea should be at a port with a Customs office (i.e. a larger port), save in emergency. Craft should fly a yellow flag until given clearance and in addition to crew's passports will need the *Ship's Certificate of Registration*. Herein can lie great difficulty.

Registration (British) of a vessel establishes title to ownership, and in theory it may be obtained after a tonnage survey and the filling-in of various forms from the Registrar of Ships. In practice the Register will not give his consent until he has established title to ownership, which involves checking through all the bills of sale, from one owner to the next, from the day of construction. With an aged vessel this can be impossible although ironically a vessel purchased from overseas is only checked from the day she enters British ownership. Over the years many owners have preferred not to bother, taking, if necessary, a useful scrap of paper obtained with far less fuss from the Royal Yachting Association.

Alas, French Customs no longer recognise the RYA document very cheerfully, and have indicated that from January 1984 owners must go through the full procedure of registration. (Until 1984 they will also accept Parts II and III of UK Customs Form C1328, provided that Part I has been lodged with the Customs before leaving the UK.) The alternatives are either to postpone one's visit (until such time as the British authorities actually institute some simpler form of listing yachts) or pay importation duty upon first arriving in France. This stands at the normal rate of Value Added Tax (TVA), currently 18.6 per cent, and in order to avoid any unnecessary surcharges it is advisable to approach a freight agent in Britain first of all. As a small consolation it may be possible to reclaim the money from the French authorities upon finally leaving France – provided you like filling in forms, sitting in dreary offices, and waiting, and waiting.

It is also useful to type out salient details of craft, engine and owner so that these may be proffered to lock-keepers who ask. Metric equivalents should be given, and the more official it all looks the better. The *Permis de Circulation*, the *Certificat de Capacité* and other documents once mandatory are at the time of writing not necessary.

Insurance certificates should be carried, confirming third-party coverage for Continental waterways. This last proviso is easy to overlook, and should be confirmed by the owner's insurance company before departing. At the time of writing it is still necessary to have a green insurance document to cover car and trailer, as supplied by motor insurance companies.

Leaving a boat in France can present problems. At present craft can only be taken into France for a period of six months in any calendar year, after which import duty must be paid. But as an alternative to leaving the country again it is possible to leave a vessel in bond, that is under Customs seal, when not in use. In the following year it may then be released for a further six months' use. This ruling does not apply for visiting craft used for hire or charter, and for these importation procedures must be complied with.

To leave a vessel in bond, the ship's papers must be deposited with the Customs, who may then put a seal on the steering equipment or part of the engine. At many ports, particularly in the South, this is a familiar business and the procedure takes a matter of minutes. But inland it can involve some negotiation with the regional Customs office, which may demand that the matter be handled by a *transporteur* or Customs agent who will apply a series of high and quite arbitrary charges for his unnecessary services.

Finding a safe spot to leave a boat in France is not easy, as navigation authorities are reluctant to take this responsibility, but with determination it is possible to leave a boat in a basin or arm under the unofficial eye of a lock-keeper. Alternatively established boatyards or hire companies may look after a vessel for a consideration.

Distances

Mileages and numbers of locks are given below for the principal routes between the English Channel and the Mediterranean. It will be noticed that routes from Calais are slightly shorter but more heavily locked. In practice the Seine is more swiftly negotiated than the canals of the North, and calculations may be adapted accordingly.

Calais—Mediterranean (Port St-Louis)

via Vitry and Marne à la Saône	1247 km (775 miles) and 235 locks
via Paris and Loing, Briare, etc	1286 km (799 miles) and 211 locks
via Paris and Canal de Bourgogne	1286 km (799 miles) and 273 locks
via Paris and Canal du Nivernais	1350 km (839 miles) and 280 locks
via Paris, Marne and Marne-Saône	1371 km (852 miles) and 209 locks

Le Havre—Mediterranean (Port St-Louis)

via Paris and Loing, Briare, etc	1338 km (832 miles) and 178 locks
via Paris and Canal de Bourgogne	1338 km (832 miles) and 240 locks
via Paris and Canal du Nivernais	1402 km (871 miles) and 247 locks
via Paris, Marne and Marne-Saône	1423 km (884 miles) and 176 locks

Closures

A schedule of intended canal closures is necessary in planning a route. Waterway repairs take place throughout the summer, but for prolonged stoppages alternative routes are usually left open. A provisional list of closures (*chômages*) is published in January and subject to representations from canal carriers, hire companies, etc a revised schedule is available by the end of March. Lists can be obtained from the French Government Tourist Office in London or the Touring Club de France in Paris.

Locks are closed on Easter Monday, May 1, July 14, November 11 and December 25. On the Canal de Bourgogne and Canal de la Marne à la Saône they are currently closed on Sundays also, while on many canals there is a lunch break from 12.00 to 12.30, or from 12.30 to 1.00 pm.

Locks are otherwise open at the following times:

January 1–31	7.30 am to 5.30 pm
February 1–28	7.00 am to 6.00 pm
March 1–31	7.00 am to 7.00 pm
April 1–September 30	6.30 am to 7.30 pm
October 1–November 30	7.00 am to 6.00 pm
December 1–31	7.30 am to 5.30 pm

On certain rivers locks are open for longer hours.

MARKERS
When going DOWNSTREAM

Left-hand markers
(leave to port)

Black or Black and
White buoy or post

Right-hand markers
(leave to starboard)

Red or Red and
White buoy or post

SIGNALS FROM BOATS

Siren signals

 (one blast)

I am turning to starboard (to my right), or

I aim to meet and pass you on the correct side,

i.e. to 'keep to the right'

Also used as a routine warning at narrows,

turns etc

(two blasts)

I am turning to port (to my left), or

I aim to meet and pass you on the 'wrong' side,

i.e. to 'keep to the left'

(repeated blasts)

Danger signal (fire, fouled tow, hooked up in

lock, etc)

Flag signals

Blue flag or board, hoisted on starboard side by
craft going upstream on certain rivers and
wishing to pass on the 'wrong' side (i.e. to
'keep to the left')
Downstream craft fly a similar signal to
acknowledge

Red flag. Boat broken down or in vulnerable
situation – please pass with care
If shown on a dredger, wait until flag
withdrawn, or pass on other side, where a red
and white flag is sometimes shown if the way
is clear

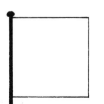

Yellow flag requests Customs clearance when
entering country

NOTICE BOARDS AND MARKERS

(NB: rectangular boards are for the waterways, circular notices for roads alongside!)

 Speed limit (k/hr)

 Sound siren

 Cross over to left

 Pass on 'wrong' side (keep left)

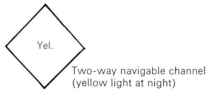 No entry (red light at night)

 No overtaking

 No overtaking beyond sign

Limite de trematage

 No overtaking (push tows only)

 Ease off please (usually when passing between lock gates)

Debrayez s'il vous plaît

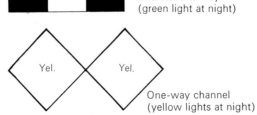 Channel this way (green light at night)

Gr. Wh. Gr.

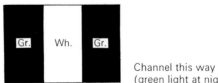 One-way channel (yellow lights at night)

Yel. Yel.

Yel. Two-way navigable channel (yellow light at night)

 No mooring

 No wash

 No passing

 End of restriction

Blue
Blue

 Channel 20 metres from bank

20

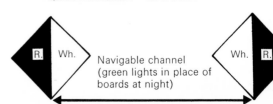 Navigable channel (green lights in place of boards at night)

R. Wh.   Wh. R.

Arthur at St-Léger, Canal du Centre

Index